A Journey to Mount Carmel

Fr. Jeffrey Kirby, S.T.D.

A Journey to Mount Carmel

A Nine-Day Preparation for Investiture in the Brown Scapular of Our Lady

SOPHIA INSTITUTE PRESS
Manchester, New Hampshire

Cover design: by LUCAS Art & Design, Jenison, MI.
Artwork: *Santísima Virgen del Carmen Cuzqueña*,
ca. 1650, Wikimedia Commons

Sophia Institute Press
Box 5284, Manchester, NH 03108
1-800-888-9344
www.SophiaInstitute.com

Sophia Institute Press is a registered trademark of Sophia Institute.

paperback ISBN 978-1-64413-544-0

ebook ISBN 978-1-64413-545-7

Library of Congress Control Number: 2022941833

First printing

To
Barbara Ternovan

Contents

A Journey to Mount Carmel

Introduction

*Let us therefore approach the throne of grace
with boldness, so that we may receive mercy
and find grace to help in time of need.*

—Hebrews 4:16

Yes, Lord!

This simple expression says it all. It is what you're saying by preparing to be invested in the Brown Scapular of Our Lady of Mount Carmel. You are affirming your own commitment to the Lord Jesus. You are fanning into flame the graces of your Baptism and affirming your personal decision for Jesus Christ.

Yes, Lord!

The Brown Scapular is not jewelry, religious sentimentality, or a misplaced act of superstition. The scapular, which is a simple collection of two pieces of cloth, is a declaration that you have put on Christ and seek to follow His way in imitation of Mary, Our Lady of Mount Carmel.

A Journey to Mount Carmel

The Power of Mount Carmel

The Church has many religious orders and several different scapulars. The Carmelite Order, however, is especially dear to the Church since its foundations started at Mount Carmel in the Holy Land. The holy mountain is a sign of the Church's call to contemplate and listen to the voice of the living God. Carmelites live this way of life. They model it for us and call us to live the same way of life. In this way, the Brown Scapular of Our Lady of Mount Carmel is especially close to the heart of the Church. The Church offers it to all the baptized, as they seek to listen to God and follow the way of the Lord Jesus.

The Commitments of the Scapular

While there are many devotional investitures in the Brown Scapular, such as at First Holy Communion Masses, these are different from the intentional and prepared investiture in the scapular.

The person who wants to be invested in the Brown Scapular must be ready to take in its commitments. These should be discerned before a person pursues formal investiture in the scapular.

The commitments of the scapular include wearing the scapular daily, praying a daily Rosary, offering up some form of fasting, seeking to serve those in need, and observing chastity according to one's state in life.

Why Prepare?

After seeing the commitments that are associated with the Brown Scapular, it becomes clear that some type of preparation is needed. It's prudent to discern and ready our hearts for such an undertaking as the scapular.

Introduction

Our fallen world is busy and it's easy to be distracted. Oftentimes the first casualty of activism is the spiritual life. A strong preparation for the investiture in the Brown Scapular could serve as a great encouragement to receiving the scapular and growing in our relationship with the Lord Jesus.

How to Prepare?

There is no formal preparation for the investiture in the Brown Scapular. The spiritual treasury of the Church has many resources and suggestions.

The first task in preparing for the scapular would be to select a holy day on which you'd like to be invested. Any holy day is good, although sometimes a feast day of the Lord or of Our Lady is preferred. Please see the appendix of this book for suggestions.

Once you've selected a holy day, you'll want to make sure a priest is available on that day. Only a priest can invest you in the Brown Scapular, and so you'll need to ensure that a priest is free to meet with you on the holy day you've chosen. You'll also want to pick a day in which you'll be able to attend Mass and receive Holy Communion. The participation in Mass and the reception of Holy Communion are essential on the day of your investiture. These should not be ignored under any circumstances.

As a help in readying yourself to receive the scapular, this book collects some of the best spiritual gifts in the treasury of the Church.

The format of this book follows the six baptismal promises. These were specifically chosen since the scapular is meant to heighten and intensify our living out of the baptismal way of life. The baptismal promises are about our consecration and commitment to Jesus Christ. As such, there is no better resource for a preparation in receiving the Brown Scapular.

In addition to the baptismal promises, the book provides other catechetical and spiritual resources as a help and inspiration to you.

The Format for the Preparation

The book has nine days of preparation. The selection of nine days is meant to provoke the devotion of a novena, a nine-day period of prayer and petition. The hope is that the preparation for the scapular will also be approached as nine days of prayer and intercession, as well as a nine-day retreat and time of renewal and rejuvenation in our relationship with the living God.

There are nine chapters of the book that follow the nine days of preparation. Each chapter has three main parts:

- Preparation: this portion consists of opening prayers and the goal of the day.
- Teachings: this part includes a series of catecheses that develop and apply the focus of the day.
- Spiritual Exercises: this portion includes an array of spiritual resources from the treasury of the Church.

Each of the parts of the book are meant to stress Christian discipleship, the Carmelite spirituality and history, and the importance of Mary in our lives.

Getting Started

With the guidance above, you are ready. Select your holy day. Organize your preparation. It's time to declare: "Yes, Lord!" Get started.

A Journey to Mount Carmel

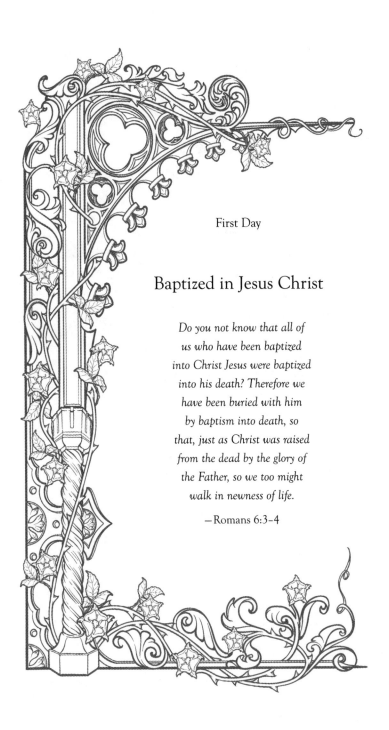

First Day

Baptized in Jesus Christ

*Do you not know that all of
us who have been baptized
into Christ Jesus were baptized
into his death? Therefore we
have been buried with him
by baptism into death, so
that, just as Christ was raised
from the dead by the glory of
the Father, so we too might
walk in newness of life.*

—Romans 6:3–4

A Journey to Mount Carmel

PREPARATION

As you start Day One, these simple preparatory acts will help you get started and keep you focused.

Today's Spiritual Goal

To understand what it truly means to be a Catholic Christian, baptized and consecrated to God.

Opening Prayers

Come, Holy Spirit, fill the hearts of Your faithful. And kindle in them the fire of Your love. Send forth Your Spirit, and they shall be created. And You will renew the face of the earth.

Lord, by the light of the Holy Spirit You have taught the hearts of Your faithful. In the same Spirit, help us to relish what is right and always rejoice in Your consolation. We ask this through Christ our Lord. Amen.

We fly to your protection, O holy Mother of God. Despise not our petitions in our necessities, but deliver us always from all dangers, O glorious and blessed Virgin. Amen.

O Blessed Mother, as we prepare to be invested in your scapular, show us what it means to be baptized in your Son. We rely on you. Amen.

TEACHINGS

After completing the simple preparatory acts, these teachings are provided so that a deeper understanding of the Christian way of life can be given and a true preparation can be made for the investiture in the Brown Scapular.

The Weight of Glory

During the pontificate of Pope St. John Paul II, a reporter asked him which of the papal titles were most significant to him. Many of us are not aware, or have become accustomed to the centuries-old titles given to the pope, such as the Bishop of Rome, the Vicar of Christ, Successor of Saint Peter, Supreme Pontiff of the Universal Church, and Sovereign of the State of Vatican City, to name just five. In addition, there are the titles of direct address, such as "Your Holiness," or "Holy Father." Imagine being addressed by such titles all throughout the day!

The reporter's question was a good one. Which of all these titles meant the most to the John Paul II?

In his usual teaching style, Pope St. John Paul II gave several answers in gradual importance. He explained how the titles summarize our Faith, and then how the titles humble him and remind him of his vocation in the Church, but then he reached the answer that truly disclosed his heart.

John Paul II answered the casual question with a profound answer. It is an answer that should shake us and remind us of our dignity as believers. Our beloved saintly pope responded that his favored title was the one that bore the greatest weight. It was the title, "Christian." For John Paul II, the most cherished of all his titles was "Christian." It is the foundation of everything else and the one that gives meaning to all else. It is the basis, the inspiration, and the declaration of everything else. I am a Christian. I am baptized into Jesus Christ. I am a child of God. I am anointed. I am "a small Christ."

> Through Baptism the Christian is sacramentally assimilated to Jesus, who in his own Baptism anticipates his death and resurrection. The Christian must enter into this mystery of humble self-abasement and repentance, go down into the water with Jesus in order to rise with him, be reborn of water and the Spirit so as to become the Father's beloved son in the Son and "walk in newness of life." — *Catechism of the Catholic Church*, 537

The title Christian, therefore, is both our greatest boast of God's grace and our most pressing challenge. In Baptism, we were made children of God and members of Christ's own Body. We were made Christians, and throughout our lives we have to work and suffer to live up to this upward calling. We pray, with St. Paul, to press on every day toward the goal for the prize of the heavenly call.

> Not that I have already obtained this or have already reached the goal; but I press on to make it my own, because Christ Jesus has made me his own. Beloved, I do not consider that I have made it my own; but this one thing I do: forgetting what lies behind and straining forward to what lies ahead, I press on toward the goal for the prize of the heavenly call of God in Christ Jesus. — Philippians 3:12–14

The early believers of our Faith, however, did not feel worthy of the title Christian. Since it implied a person being "a small Christ," they avoided the title. The earliest believers of the Lord Jesus were simply identified as "followers of the Way." The expression indicated that believers understood their call to live and continue the Way of the Lord Jesus. Over time, however, unbelievers who witnessed the love and selfless service of our forefathers and foremothers began to call them Christians. And so, it was those outside of the Faith who began to call us Christians, since they saw something of the Lord Jesus in the followers of the Way (cf. Acts 11:26). The title eventually stuck and we now call ourselves Christian. We should never forget, however, the meaning and demands that come with such a name and the humility of our forebears in approaching such a name.

St. Paul understood the gravity of what it meant to be a Christian. He refers to "an eternal weight of glory" that will be given to us in Heaven and for which we yearn and readily suffer for the sake of the gospel in this life.

> So we do not lose heart. Even though our outer nature is wasting away, our inner nature is being renewed day by day. For this slight momentary affliction is preparing us for an eternal weight of glory beyond all measure, because we look not at what can be seen but at what cannot be seen; for what can be seen is temporary, but what cannot be seen is eternal. — 2 Corinthians 4:16-18

Baptism is an eternal weight of glory. By Baptism, we became members of Christ's own Body. It is how we can dare to call ourselves Christians. We now live, move, and have our being in Jesus Christ. As such, we draw close to Him, allow His grace to transform us, we seek to faithfully follow His way, to continue His work, to love as He loved, and to share eternal glory with Him in eternity (see Acts 17:28; 1 Cor. 12:31; 13:11-13).

As Pope St. John Paul II indicated, we carry the title, the name, of Christian on our shoulders and in our hearts. It is our most esteemed and pressing title, and so we are summoned every day to fulfill and live up to the glorious name of Christian.

Have I taken the name Christian for granted? Do I understand what it means and the way of life to which I'm called by accepting such a name?

Sanctifying Grace and Newness of Life

Before the Fall of our first parents, humanity held sanctifying grace. It is a filial, familial relationship with God. It is the grace that gives us supernatural life and justifies us to be partakers of the divine nature, to be an adopted son or daughter of God, and so an heir to eternal life.

In the Fall, sanctifying grace was lost. It was not restored to humanity until the Paschal Mystery of the Lord Jesus, namely, until His Passion, Death, and Resurrection.

> But the free gift is not like the trespass. For if the many died through the one man's trespass, much more surely have the grace of God and the free gift in the grace of the one man, Jesus Christ, abounded for the many. — Romans 5:15

From the Paschal Mystery of the Lord Jesus, we have seven sacraments. The first sacrament, and the one that initially restores sanctifying grace, is Holy Baptism. As sanctifying grace might be lost to grave sin, it is restored by the sacraments of Penance (Confession) and/or the Anointing of the Sick. The other four sacraments—Confirmation, Holy Communion, Holy Matrimony, and Holy Orders—nourish and enrich sanctifying grace within us.

In Baptism, therefore, we first receive the great spiritual treasure of sanctifying grace. Our spiritual tradition also calls this *deifying grace or habitual grace*. It is called deifying grace since it literally makes us "like God" in Jesus Christ. It is also called habitual grace since it dwells within us, it takes up a habitation—a residence—in our souls.

Once sanctifying grace dwells within us, we are born to newness of life—to divine life—and are guided by God along the path of glory unto glory.

> Now the Lord is the Spirit, and where the Spirit of the Lord is, there is freedom. And all of us, with unveiled faces, seeing the glory of the Lord as though reflected in a mirror, are being transformed into the same image from one degree of glory to another; for this comes from the Lord, the Spirit.—2 Corinthians 3:17–18

Do I realize the immense gift of sanctifying grace in my life? Do I seek to nurture this grace in my life by a frequent and worthy reception of the sacraments?

The Scapular and Clothing Ourselves in Jesus Christ

As we receive and nurture sanctifying grace in our souls, we are strengthened to follow the way of the Lord Jesus. St. Paul describes this as being "clothed" in Jesus Christ. The figurative language is meant to express not only an external adherence to Jesus Christ, but an internal surrender to the workings of His grace in our lives.

> As many of you as were baptized into Christ have clothed yourselves with Christ.—Galatians 3:27

The imagery is helpful as we reflect upon our Baptism, our status as the children of God, our esteemed name of *Christian*, and the reliving of the Paschal Mystery of Jesus Christ and the dwelling of His grace within us. Imprisoned and preparing to die for the Lord Jesus, St. Paul reminds us of our Christian vocation:

> I therefore, the prisoner in the Lord, beg you to lead a life worthy of the calling to which you have been called, with all humility and gentleness, with patience, bearing with one another in love, making every effort to maintain the unity of the Spirit in the bond of peace. There is one body and one Spirit, just as you were called to the one hope of your call-ing, one Lord, one faith, one baptism, one God and Father of all, who is above all and through all and in all. — Ephesians 4:1-6

The imagery of being clothed in Jesus Christ and living ac-cording to His way of life is also helpful as we seek to understand the pious tradition of the scapular, since a scapular is a piece of clothing (or an abbreviated piece of clothing) that is worn as a sacramental on our bodies.

Outside of our spiritual tradition, the word *scapular* refers to anything relating to our shoulders or shoulder blades. Within our religious tradition, therefore, the clothing that covers the shoulders has come to traditionally be called a scapular. Full scapulars were initially worn by Carmelite Friars and Sisters (and other religious orders) to cover their habits. Scapulars were worn during times of labor or strenuous work projects so that the habit of the Religious would not be torn or dirtied. Eventually, the scapular itself became acclimated as a part of the habit.

In the course of time, baptized lay Christians saw the spirituality and work of the Carmelite Order and wanted to participate in it. The Carmelite spirituality focuses on an active listening to God, the practice of contemplation, and on a deep love for the Mother of God. These spiritual aspects greatly inspired many Christians to deepen in their own commitment to the Lord Jesus. As such, they sought to follow the Carmelites on the way of the Lord.

Such an accompaniment with the Carmelites led to the laity taking on a small form of the scapular themselves. Such a scapular consists of two small cloth squares joined by shoulder tapes and worn under a person's clothing along their chest and back. It was a small sign of their baptismal consecration to Jesus Christ through His Blessed Mother within the contemplative tradition of the ancient Carmelite way of life.

The Brown Scapular is not jewelry. It is not an accessory to our clothing. It is not a good luck or other magical charm. The Brown Scapular is a sign of our baptismal consecration to Jesus Christ. It is a revered sacramental within the Christian tradition. It symbolizes the convictions of our heart and represents the greatest aspirations of our lives: we belong to Christ. We seek to live Christ. We labor to share Christ. These are the messages of the Brown Scapular.

Do I understand that the scapular is a sign of my consecration to Jesus Christ? Do I let the scapular remind and convict me of my responsibilities as a disciple of the Lord Jesus?

> Above all, clothe yourselves with love, which binds everything together in perfect harmony. And let the peace of Christ rule in your hearts, to which indeed you were called in the one body. And be thankful. Let the word of Christ dwell in you richly; teach

> and admonish one another in all wisdom; and with gratitude in your hearts sing psalms, hymns, and spiritual songs to God. And whatever you do, in word or deed, do everything in the name of the Lord Jesus, giving thanks to God the Father through him. —Colossians 3:14-17

Mary, Co-Redemptrix

In recognizing our call as Christians to relive the Paschal Mystery of the Lord Jesus, especially as it's represented in the wearing of the Brown Scapular, we are aware of the presence and spiritual motherhood of the Blessed Virgin Mary.

Mary is truly the Lady of the Paschal Mystery. She is the Woman spoken of in the *Protoevangelium*, the first promise of a Savior given to humanity.

> I will put enmity between you and the woman, and between your offspring and hers; he will strike your head, and you will strike his heel. —Genesis 3:15

At the beginning of time, after the Fall of our first parents, the living God gave the human family the promise of a Savior. The promise—the spiritual *Protoevangelium*, that is, the "first gospel"—was our only hope. It gave encouragement to humanity as the consequences of sin befell us.

> After his fall, man was not abandoned by God. On the contrary, God calls him and in a mysterious way heralds the coming victory over evil and his restoration from his fall. This passage in Genesis is called the *Protoevangelium*

> ("first gospel"): the first announcement of the Messiah and Redeemer, of a battle between the serpent and the Woman, and of the final victory of a descendant of hers.—*Catechism of the Catholic Church*, 410

For prophecy to be fulfilled, therefore, there would be a Woman, a Savior, a victory, and suffering. In addressing the Evil One, the ancient foe, the living God explains:

- a Woman, "I will put enmity between you and the woman"
- a Savior, "and between your offspring and hers"
- a victory, "He will strike at your head"
- and suffering, "and you will strike at his heel"

There is absolutely only one Savior, one Mediator between God and man. The Woman of the promise would be the first to declare, insist, and defend the one Savior, the one Mediator. As we see by prophecy, however, the one Savior will be closely connected to the Woman of the promise, who is His Mother. She will intimately accompany Him and be a vital part of His saving work and redemptive suffering for the salvation of humanity.

> This is right and is acceptable in the sight of God our Savior, who desires everyone to be saved and to come to the knowledge of the truth. For there is one God; there is also one mediator between God and humankind, Christ Jesus, himself human, who gave himself a ransom for all—this was attested at the right time.—1 Timothy 2:3-6

The one Savior was revealed to us. Jesus of Nazareth is the one Mediator between God and man. He fulfilled all the prophecies and promises of the Old Testament. He is the long-awaited, Anointed Savior. And so, his Mother is the Woman of the promise. As the Lord Jesus fulfills the *Protoevangelium*, so does His Mother. From the first moment of her Immaculate Conception, Mary was prepared for this vocation. As we see throughout salvation history, Mary was blessed and strengthened to faithfully and generously fulfill her essential maternal role in salvation history.

> And the child's father and mother were amazed at what was being said about him. Then Simeon blessed them and said to his mother Mary, "This child is destined for the falling and the rising of many in Israel, and to be a sign that will be opposed so that the inner thoughts of many will be revealed—and a sword will pierce your own soul too."—Luke 2:33–35

Mary is the Woman united to the one Savior. She spiritually walks with the Lord Jesus and suffers through His Passion and Death with Him. We see her at Calvary:

> When Jesus saw his mother and the disciple whom he loved standing beside her, he said to his mother, "Woman, here is your son." Then he said to the disciple, "Here is your mother." And from that hour the disciple took her into his own home.—John 19:26–27

Mary is the Savior's Mother. She is the Lady of the Paschal Mystery. She is the Woman of the promise. She is the Co-Redemptrix with her Son, Jesus Christ, our one, sole Redeemer.

She is also our Mother. As with Mary, therefore, so with each of us. We are called to declare Mary as our true Mother and to join in her accompaniment and proximity with the Lord Jesus in His Paschal Mystery.

Do I see Mary as closely connected to the saving work of the Lord Jesus? Do I ask Mary to help me relive the Paschal Mystery of the Lord Jesus in my own life?

SPIRITUAL EXERCISES

After finishing the teachings for today, the following spiritual exercises are provided. The exercises are the heart of the daily preparation for the investiture in the Brown Scapular. Not all of these exercises must be done. They are provided as a small treasure chest for your spiritual preparation.

Examination of Conscience

This examination of conscience can help with your general moral awareness of what it means to follow the Lord Jesus. In addition, it is strongly recommended that you go to Confession during your time of preparation.

- Do I understand the weight of glory that comes with being a Christian?
- Do I realize what it means to declare myself a Christian?
- Do I seek to be a universal brother or sister to all people?
- Do I seek the grace of the Paschal Mystery against the fears and temptations of my life?
- Do I avoid suffering?
- Do I nurture a comfortable and easy life away from the Cross of the Lord?
- Do I value the gift of my Baptism?
- Do I worthily receive Holy Communion as often as I can?
- Do I frequently go to Confession and seek the help of God's grace?
- Have I spiritually accepted Mary as my Mother?

Praying the Holy Mass

As the summit and source of the Christian way of life, reflect upon the Holy Mass. In particular, pray over the minor absolution: "May Almighty God have mercy on us, forgive us our sins, and bring us to everlasting life."

Consider: (1) The baptismal tone of the minor absolution; (2) God's desire to remove our sins and save us from darkness; (3) God's invitation for us to share everlasting life with Him, although we do not merit it nor could we ever deserve it.

Marian Devotion: The Seven Sorrows of Mary

1. The prophecy of Simeon
2. The flight into Egypt
3. The loss of the Child Jesus in the temple
4. The meeting of Jesus and Mary on the Way of the Cross
5. The Crucifixion
6. The taking down of the Body of Jesus from the Cross
7. The burial of Jesus.

Divine Wisdom: The Beatitudes

Blessed are the poor in spirit, for theirs is the kingdom of heaven. Blessed are those who mourn, for they will be comforted. Blessed are the meek, for they will inherit the earth. Blessed are those who hunger and thirst for righteousness, for they will be filled. Blessed are the merciful, for they will receive mercy. Blessed are the pure in heart, for they will see God. Blessed are the peacemakers, for they will be called children of God. Blessed are those who are persecuted for righteousness' sake, for theirs is the kingdom of Heaven. (Matt. 5:3–10)

Three Optional Prayer Methods

1. Lectio Divina

Spend some time, perhaps even fifteen minutes, repeating and breathing into your heart the following portion of the living Word of God: "I have been crucified with Christ; and it is no longer I who live, but it is Christ who lives in me. And the life I now live in the flesh I live by faith in the Son of God, who loved me and gave himself for me" (Gal. 2:19b–20).

Consider: The disciple and apostle, St. Paul, seeking to relive the Paschal Mystery in his life and reflecting on the transformative work of grace in his soul. Reflect on how God desires for you to relive the Passion, Death, and Resurrection of Jesus Christ in your life. Evaluate the different expectations and opportunities of your life. Ask for the grace to see what God wants of you. Rely on the Paschal Mystery. Seek the transformation of grace.

2. Composition of Place Meditation

Enter into a contemplation of place. Use your spiritual imagination and compose a place. Imagine the sights, smells, sounds, taste, and touch of the environment. Allow yourself to be truly, spiritually present in that moment.

Compose the scene in the Jerusalem Temple when the Christ Child is presented to His father in the ancient ceremony of His people. Smell the incense of the holy place. Hear the sounds of whispered prayers. Watch as Simeon approaches. See the old man's wrinkles, his slow pace, his frayed beard. Feel the calloused hands of Simeon as he pats you on the back and prepares to hold the Christ Child. Watch the amazement of Mary and Joseph at what was being said about the Christ Child. Hear the broken voice of the esteemed elder. Smell the animals being readied for sacrifice. Look upon the Christ Child and open your heart to Him. Speak to Him. Declare Him your Lord. See Luke 2:33–35.

3. Poustinia Meditation

Unlike others methods of prayer, the task of the Poustinia Meditation is to clear your mind of all thoughts and attempt to think of nothing other than a simple word or expression. We can remain quiet and wait for a word to be given to us, or we can select a word before our time of prayer. The word or expression, whether given or selected, is repeated multiple times or simply held in our minds. Sometimes the use of a foreign word can help us stay focused. For our exercise today, we can use Paschal Mystery, or oblation, or Calvary.

Suggested Saints and Holy Ones

As Christians, we are surrounded by "a cloud of witnesses"—the saints and holy ones in heaven who intercede and help us. On this first day of our preparation, we can turn to Pope St. Telesphorus. He was the eighth pope. He was one of the early Christian hermits from Mount Carmel. He was a man of deep prayer and strong doctrine. He fought against false beliefs and called the Church back to her spiritual roots. He died a martyr and is an example to us of love and fidelity.

Stations of the Cross Suggestion

The Stations of the Cross are recommended. They can all be prayed or simply the Fourth Station: Jesus Meets His Mother. Reflect upon the love between the Savior and His Mother as they share in the work of God. Ask for the grace to relive the Paschal Mystery and faithfully cooperate with God's plan for your life.

Rosary Suggestion

The Rosary is always recommended. Today, the Luminous Mysteries are suggested. In particular, the First Mystery of the Baptism of the Lord is proposed. Reflect on your sharing in the Baptism of the Lord, especially as it's fulfilled in His Paschal Mystery.

Three Traditional Prayers

Act of Faith

O my God, I firmly believe that You are one God in three Divine Persons—Father, Son, and Holy Spirit. I believe that Your divine Son became man and died for our sins and that He will come to judge the living and the dead. I believe these and all the truths which the Holy Catholic Church teaches because You have revealed them Who are eternal truth and wisdom, Who can neither deceive nor be deceived. In this faith I intend to live and die. Amen.

Breastplate of St. Patrick

Christ be with me, Christ within me, Christ behind me, Christ before me, Christ beside me, Christ to win me, Christ to comfort and restore me. Christ beneath me, Christ above me, Christ in quiet, Christ in danger, Christ in hearts of all that love me, Christ in mouth of friend and stranger. Amen.

Prayer for Renewal of Heart by St. John Henry Newman

O my Lord, give me that purity of conscience which alone can receive Your inspirations. My ears are dull, so that I cannot hear Your voice. My eyes are dim, so that I cannot see Your presence. You alone can quicken my hearing, and purge my sight, and cleanse and renew my heart. Teach me, like Mary, to sit at Your feet, and to hear Your Word. Amen.

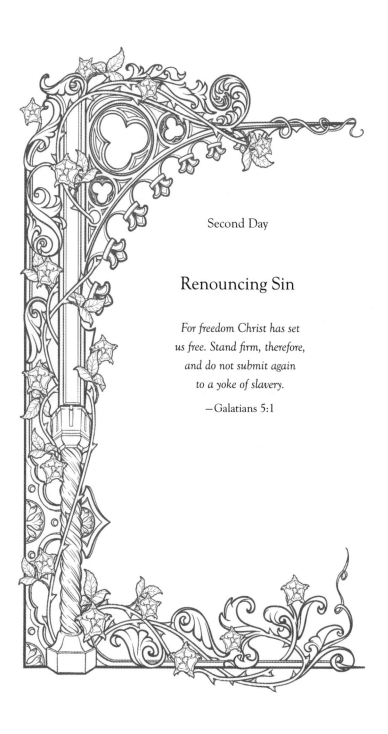

Second Day

Renouncing Sin

For freedom Christ has set
us free. Stand firm, therefore,
and do not submit again
to a yoke of slavery.

—Galatians 5:1

PREPARATION

As you start Day Two, these simple preparatory acts will help you get started and keep you focused.

Today's Spiritual Goal:

To understand my first baptismal promise: "Do you renounce sin, so as to live in the freedom of the children of God?"

Opening Prayers

Come, Holy Spirit, fill the hearts of Your faithful. And kindle in them the fire of Your love. Send forth Your Spirit, and they shall be created. And You will renew the face of the earth.

Lord, by the light of the Holy Spirit You have taught the hearts of Your faithful. In the same Spirit, help us to relish what is right and always rejoice in Your consolation. We ask this through Christ our Lord. Amen.

We fly to your protection, O holy Mother of God. Despise not our petitions in our necessities, but deliver us always from all dangers, O glorious and blessed Virgin. Amen.

O Blessed Mother, as we prepare to be invested in your scapular, show us the wickedness of sin and the glory of true freedom in your beloved Son. We rely on you. Amen.

Teachings

After completing the simple preparatory acts, these teachings are provided so that a deeper understanding of the Christian way of life can be given and a true preparation can be made for the investiture in the Brown Scapular.

Renouncing Sin and Working Out Our Salvation

Years ago, I had a friend who tragically had a long-standing addiction to drugs. The drugs held a dominion over his life. He was enslaved to them and the chemical high they gave him. He overdosed several times and on several occasions was rushed to the hospital. On one such occasion, it was feared that he would die.

The man survived and vowed to change. It was a powerful conversion and a desire for transformation in his life. He was sent to a rehabilitation center. Later he recalled that for the first few days of his recovery, he was in intense detoxification. He described how his body shook, jerked, and twisted violently. He had no control. The man could not even manage his own body, and he felt that he had lost everything.

The friend shared with me that the only words that kept going through his mind throughout his entire ordeal were from St. Paul: "Work out your own salvation with fear and trembling."

> Therefore, my beloved, just as you have always obeyed me, not only in my presence, but much more now in my absence, work out your own salvation with fear and trembling; for it is God who is at work in you, enabling you both to will and to work for his good pleasure. — Philippians 2:12–13

After my friend passed through his detoxification, he still had a long road of healing and restoration to undergo, but the initial break from the slavery of sin had begun. He was beginning to know and experience the freedom of the children of God.

In our own lives, we are also called to recognize the slavery of sin and seek our independence in Jesus Christ. Sin wants to imprison us and isolate us from God and those we love. Sin is a fierce enemy. We must constantly be on guard and work to keep our hearts free from the stains and wounds of sin.

St. Paul continues and describes the process by which the "old person" of sin gives way to the "new person" in Jesus Christ. He writes:

> We know that our old self was crucified with him so that the body of sin might be destroyed, and we might no longer be enslaved to sin. — Romans 6:6

And St. Paul observes:

> For those who live according to the flesh set their minds on the things of the flesh, but those who live according to the Spirit set their minds on the things of the Spirit.... for if you live according to the flesh, you will die; but if by the Spirit you put to death the deeds of the body, you will live. — Romans 8:5, 13

Do I realize my own addiction to sin? Do I want Jesus Christ to work out His salvation in my own life?

The Deception and Slavery of Sin

As fallen human beings, we've become accustomed to sin. We can easily forget that we were not made for sin. We can undervalue what it robs from us.

Sin is a privation of being, which means it diminishes who we are. It eats away our existence and the goodness of creation. It is not human or real, but is actually antihuman and anti-reality. Sin diminishes what exists. It degrades us and is a decay to our humanity. It makes us strangers to ourselves and the world around us. Sin steals what does not belong to it. It robs us of the richness of life and the goodness of our humanity. Sin is a spirit of darkness. It lies, deceives, and manipulates goodness, truth, and beauty. Sin promises false blessings and works to enslave us in its treachery and duplicity.

> Everyone who commits sin is guilty of lawlessness; sin is lawlessness. — 1 John 3:4

Sin is an existential calamity and a blight on our personal identity. When we sin, we lose a part of ourselves and become less of the person God has created us to be. St. Paul addresses this consequence of sin and calls us to seek a "full stature" in Jesus Christ.

> The gifts he gave were that some would be apostles, some prophets, some evangelists, some pastors and teachers, to equip the saints for the work of ministry, for building up the body of Christ, until all of us come to the unity of the faith and of the knowledge of the Son of God, to maturity, to the measure of the full stature of Christ. — Ephesians 4:11–13

As we seek our full stature in Jesus Christ and labor to be purged from sin, we are challenged by St. Paul who describes for us the sacrifice that must be made for God's grace to work:

> And those who belong to Christ Jesus have crucified the flesh with its passions and desires. —Galatians 5:24

St. Paul continues:

> May I never boast of anything except the cross of our Lord Jesus Christ, by which the world has been crucified to me, and I to the world. —Galatians 6:14

The call is given to us. We must renounce sin, its slavery, and fallen kingdom. We must strive to live and persevere in the freedom won for us by Jesus Christ.

Have I become accustomed to sin and forgotten its consequences on my existence and personal identity? Do I fight to keep sin away from my soul?

The Freedom of God's Children

In Jesus Christ, we have a power given to us, a power to find grace within our fallen world and to cooperate with it. This is true freedom.

Properly understood, freedom is the power to do what is right and good. Freedom liberates us from passing fads, our fallen desires, wayward inclinations, and fallen areas of life. With our freedom, we can soar above such things and see and do what is good, true, and beautiful. Freedom teaches us that sin doesn't define us. It has no power over us, except the power we give it. We are free when we choose goodness and holiness in our lives.

> For you were called to freedom, brothers and sisters; only do not use your freedom as an opportunity for

self-indulgence, but through love become slaves to
one another. — Galatians 5:13

In our culture today, however, freedom is abused, poorly taught,
and is given an incomplete definition. For some, freedom is simply the
license to do whatever they want. There are no norms of goodness, no
obligation to truth, and no care for others. People who live by such a
fallen view of freedom live only for themselves and their own desires
and wants. It is a recipe for selfishness, destruction, and misery.

Freedom is the power, rooted in reason and will,
to act or not to act, to do this or that, and so to
perform deliberate actions on one's own responsibility. By free will one shapes one's own life. Human
freedom is a force for growth and maturity in truth
in goodness; it attains its perfection when directed
toward God, our beatitude. — *Catechism of the Catholic Church*, 1731

As the children of God, who are being saved in Jesus Christ
and who have received the Holy Spirit, we are called to live according to freedom. The Christian way of life is one of freedom.
The Spirit dwells within us, stirs us, and strengthens us to live in
the freedom of God's children.

Now the Lord is the Spirit, and where the Spirit of
the Lord is, there is freedom. — 2 Corinthians 3:17

Do I reject the slavery of sin? Do I prize the freedom I have
received in Jesus Christ and do whatever I can to strengthen and
nurture it?

A Journey to Mount Carmel

Mount Carmel and Our Spiritual Freedom

The life of freedom helps us to defer to truth, suffer for goodness, and celebrate beauty. Such movements of our hearts are reflected and nourished in sacred places.

Of the many sacred places within the Christian tradition, Mount Carmel shines out as a holy place of prayer and spiritual freedom. The joy of our interior freedom is given expression in the revered and sacred place of Mount Carmel.

Mount Carmel is one of the most impressive physical features of the Holy Land. Rather than just one mountain, it is actually a mountain range that spans some twenty-four miles along the northwestern to the southeastern portion of the Holy Land. Due to its sources of irrigation, Mount Carmel is known for its life-giving vegetation and soul-rejuvenating beauty. As such, the name *Carmel* rightly means "God's vineyard" or "God's garden."

Mount Carmel, therefore, has been a place of deep mystical significance, spiritual liberation, and veneration throughout salvation history. It is particularly connected to Elijah, the Fire of God and the father of all prophets.

Mount Carmel is praised throughout the Sacred Scriptures for its beauty and splendor. It is a powerful source of grace and spiritual freedom.

The prophet Isaiah spoke of Mount Carmel:

> The wilderness and the dry land shall be glad, the desert shall rejoice and blossom; like the crocus it shall blossom abundantly, and rejoice with joy and singing. The glory of Lebanon shall be given to it, the majesty of Carmel and Sharon. They shall see the glory of the LORD, the majesty of our God. — Isaiah 35:1–2

King Solomon used the symbol of Mount Carmel to describe the attractiveness of his beloved's hair:

> Your head crowns you like Carmel, and your flowing locks are like purple; a king is held captive in the tresses. — Song of Songs 7:5

The physical splendor of Mount Carmel is celebrated because it's closely connected to its mystical and spiritual power. Mount Carmel stands as a place of safety, comfort, and beauty. These features are not only in the physical world, but also in the spiritual world.

For those Christians who seek, love, and live in the freedom of God's children, Mount Carmel is their mountain. It is their sacred place of prayer and spiritual liberation. The heart that yearns for freedom is a heart that is interiorly turned to Mount Carmel and readily finds a home there in the midst of its valleys.

It is no surprise that God would bless His Church with a scapular in honor of Our Lady of Mount Carmel and welcome all believers to renew their consecration to the Lord Jesus through such a devotion.

Do I guard the freedom of my heart? Do I seek to nurture my spiritual freedom by forming a Mount Carmel in my own soul?

Mary Immaculate

In understanding the freedom offered to us in Jesus Christ, we can turn to the exemplar of this freedom. We can reverently and rightly turn to Mary, our Immaculate Mother. In recognizing the hurt and harm of sin, the living God spared Our Lady from all stain of sin.

> In the sixth month the angel Gabriel was sent by God to a town in Galilee called Nazareth, to a virgin

> engaged to a man whose name was Joseph, of the
> house of David. The virgin's name was Mary. And he
> came to her and said, "Greetings, favored one! The
> Lord is with you." But she was much perplexed by his
> words and pondered what sort of greeting this might
> be. The angel said to her, "Do not be afraid, Mary,
> for you have found favor with God." —Luke 1:26–30

Sin would have diminished Mary and her ability to serve as the Mother of the God-Man, our long-awaited Anointed Savior. And so, free from sin, she was able to fight against sin and evil. Rather than have an easy life, or one without tension or strife, Our Lady was on the front line of the enmity between God and the Evil One, between grace and pride, between redemption and damnation. Our Lady suffered more since there was constant perseverance and consistent battles against the assaults and seductions of the Evil One. Rather than a passive presence, Our Lady was the great champion of grace and the stalwart Lady-Warrior of freedom.

From her conception in the womb, Mary was free and was molded and prepared to fulfill her vocation as the Mother of God and Mother of the Church. Such a reality was hailed by the Lord Jesus Himself:

> While he was saying this, a woman in the crowd
> raised her voice and said to him, "Blessed is the
> womb that bore you and the breasts that nursed
> you!" But he said, "Blessed rather are those who
> hear the word of God and obey it!" —Luke 11:27–28

Mary was not only a biological mother to the Lord Jesus, as esteemed as such a vocation is, but was also the First Disciple of her divine Son. She fed Him with her maternal milk, but was fed by Him with divine truth. Reflecting her perpetual state of interior freedom, Mary heard the word of God and obeyed it. In the biblical account, the Lord Jesus is giving His Mother a double act of praise.

> And Mary said, "My soul magnifies the Lord, and my spirit rejoices in God my Savior." —Luke 1:46-47

Mary is our Immaculate Mother. She is Mother and First Disciple of the Lord and Mother and Witness to each of us. We turn to her and ask for her intercession and care as we seek to renounce sin and live in the freedom of God's children.

Do I turn to Mary in difficult moments and ask for her help? Do I understand Mary as the First Disciple and as a model for us in living and persevering in freedom?

SPIRITUAL EXERCISES

After finishing the teachings for today, the following spiritual exercises are provided. The exercises are the heart of the daily preparation for the investiture in the Brown Scapular. Not all of these exercises must be done. They are provided as a small treasure chest for your spiritual preparation.

Examination of Conscience

This examination of conscience can help with your general moral awareness of what it means to follow the Lord Jesus. In addition, it is strongly recommended that you go to Confession during your time of preparation.

- ◆ Am I aware of the great spiritual consequences of sin?
- ◆ Do I regularly fight against temptations and the lies of sin?
- ◆ Do I avoid occasions of sin?
- ◆ Have I been an accomplice to the sins of others?
- ◆ Do I nurture my spiritual freedom by active prayer?
- ◆ Do I guard the interior freedom of those under my care?
- ◆ Do I honor holy places and what they represent?
- ◆ Have I created an interior Carmel in my own heart?
- ◆ Do I include Mary in my discipleship?
- ◆ Do I appeal to Mary Immaculate as a help in my fight for freedom?

Praying the Holy Mass

As the summit and source of the Christian way of life, reflect upon the Holy Mass. In particular, pray over the *Domine, non sum dignus*: "Lord, I am not worthy that you should enter under my roof, but only say the word and my soul shall be healed."

Consider: (1) the Lordship of Jesus Christ, (2) the loss of our freedom and the harm caused to us by sin, and (3) the desire for God to heal us and restore us to freedom and holiness.

Marian Devotion: The Magnificat (Luke 1:46–55)

My soul magnifies the Lord, and my spirit rejoices in God my Savior, for he has looked with favor on the lowliness of his servant. Surely, from now on all generations will call me blessed; for the Mighty One has done great things for me, and holy is his name. His mercy is for those who fear him from generation to generation. He has shown strength with his arm; he has scattered the proud in the thoughts of their hearts. He has brought down the powerful from their thrones, and lifted up the lowly; he has filled the hungry with good things, and sent the rich away empty. He has helped his servant Israel, in remembrance of his mercy, according to the promise he made to our ancestors, to Abraham and to his descendants forever.

Divine Wisdom: The Seven Gifts of the Holy Spirit

Wisdom, understanding, counsel, fortitude, knowledge, piety, and fear of the Lord.

Three Optional Prayer Methods

1. Lectio Divina

Spend some time, perhaps even fifteen minutes, repeating and breathing into your heart the following portion of the living Word of God: "Then Mary said, 'Here am I, the servant of the Lord; let it be with me according to your word.'" (Luke 1:38)

Consider: Mary sitting in prayer with a free heart actively listening as the archangel Gabriel speaks to her. Reflect on the freedom on your own heart and on how God desires to speak to you. Evaluate where you stand in your spiritual freedom. Ask for the grace to be truly free and to live by the moral law and movements of the Holy Spirit.

2. Composition of Place Meditation

Enter into a contemplation of place. Use your spiritual imagination and compose a place. Imagine the sights, smells, sounds, taste, and touch of the environment. Allow yourself to be truly, spiritually present in that moment.

Compose the scene of Mary being greeted by her kinswoman Elizabeth. Smell the food being cooked in the background as Mary arrives. Hear the sounds of animals and neighbors. Watch as Elizabeth approaches Our Lady. See the old woman's smile and her grey hair. Feel the woman's touch as she embraces Our Lady. See her tears. Feel her joy as the baby moves in her womb. Watch the shared amazement of the two women—a virgin and one thought to be barren—as they rejoice over God's actions among them. Look upon the womb of Our Lady and the preborn Christ. Open your heart to Him. Speak to Him. Declare Him your Lord. See Luke 1:39-45.

3. Poustinia Meditation

Unlike others methods of prayer, the task of the Poustinia Meditation is to clear your mind of all thoughts and attempt to think of nothing other than a simple word or expression. We can remain quiet and wait for a word to be given to us, or we can select a word before our time of prayer. The word or expression, whether given or selected, is repeated multiple times or simply held in our minds. Sometimes the use of a foreign word can help us stay focused. For our exercise today, we can use freedom, *or* spiritual crucifixion, *or* fullness in Christ.

Suggested Saints and Holy Ones

As Christians, we are surrounded by "a cloud of witnesses"—the saints and holy ones in Heaven who intercede and help us. On this second day of our preparation, we can turn to St. Maria Goretti.

As a young child, when an aggressor wanted her to submit to sexual sin and threatened her life, she firmly told him: "No, no, it is a sin!" She did not want her aggressor to commit sin and was concerned about the majesty of God, her salvation, and that of her aggressor. She was attacked and brutally murdered for her defense of virtue. She died a holy death and eventually won the conversion of her aggressor before God. In our lives, when sin threatens us and wants us to be fearful, we can turn to St. Maria Goretti and ask for her intercession.

Stations of the Cross Suggestion

The Stations of the Cross are recommended. They can all be prayed or simply the First Station: Jesus Is Condemned to Death. Reflect upon the Lord's love for you. He accepted condemnation and suffered the Passion for your salvation. Ask for the grace to remain free from sin and to live always in the freedom of the children of God.

Rosary Suggestion

The Rosary is always recommended. Today, the Sorrowful Mysteries are suggested. In particular, the First Mystery of the Agony in the Garden is proposed. Reflect on your spiritual battle against sin and your desire to love the Lord Jesus with your whole self.

Three Traditional Prayers

Act of Love

O my God, I love You above all things with my whole heart and soul, because You are all good and worthy of all my love. I love my neighbor as myself for the love of You. I forgive all who have injured me and I ask pardon of those whom I have injured. Amen.

A Journey to Mount Carmel

Prayer Before a Crucifix

Look down upon me, good and gentle Jesus while before Your face I humbly kneel and, with burning soul, pray and beseech you to fix deep in my heart lively sentiments of faith, hope, and charity; true contrition for my sins, and a firm purpose of amendment. I contemplate, with great love and tender pity, Your five most precious wounds, pondering over them within me and calling to mind the words which David, Your prophet, said to You, my Jesus: "They have pierced My hands and My feet, they have numbered all My bones."

Guardian Angel Prayer

Angel of God, my guardian dear, to whom God's love commits me here, ever this day, be at my side, to light and guard, to rule and guide. Amen.

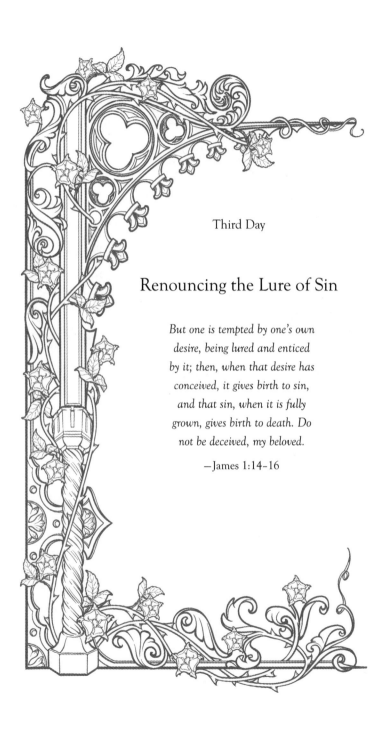

Third Day

Renouncing the Lure of Sin

*But one is tempted by one's own
desire, being lured and enticed
by it; then, when that desire has
conceived, it gives birth to sin,
and that sin, when it is fully
grown, gives birth to death. Do
not be deceived, my beloved.*

—James 1:14–16

A Journey to Mount Carmel

Preparation

As you start Day Three, these simple preparatory acts will help you get started and keep you focused.

Today's Spiritual Goal:

To understand my second baptismal promise: "Do you renounce the lure of evil, so that sin may have no mastery over you?"

Opening Prayers

Come, Holy Spirit, fill the hearts of Your faithful. And kindle in them the fire of Your love. Send forth Your Spirit, and they shall be created. And You will renew the face of the earth.

Lord, by the light of the Holy Spirit You have taught the hearts of Your faithful. In the same Spirit, help us to relish what is right and always rejoice in Your consolation. We ask this through Christ our Lord. Amen.

We fly to your protection, O holy Mother of God. Despise not our petitions in our necessities, but deliver us always from all dangers, O glorious and blessed Virgin. Amen.

O Blessed Mother, as we prepare to be invested in your scapular, help us to avoid the lure of evil and live in the freedom of God's children. We rely on you. Amen.

TEACHINGS

After completing the simple preparatory acts, these teachings are provided so that a deeper understanding of the Christian way of life can be given and a true preparation can be made for the investiture in the Brown Scapular.

Concupiscence and the Lure of Evil

Very often in our fallen world, we do not call things what they are. When it comes to the iniquity of sin, we cannot be coy. We must speak plainly and clearly. Here is the truth: Sin is a liar. Evil is deceptive. Darkness manipulates truth and goodness. And yet, we are inclined to listen to sin, accept the lies and half-truths of deception, and willingly follow the path of manipulation. This inclination toward evil, and its parallel avoidance of goodness, is a consequence of our fallen nature. Our hearts are fallen. They lie to us and accept the false promises of sin. This is what our theological tradition calls concupiscence.

> The heart is devious above all else; it is perverse—who can understand it?—Jeremiah 17:9

As shocking as it can be, we can be turned toward evil, even though we know it's evil. In such moments, we allow our desires and our intellect to be overwhelmed by the pleasure of perceived joy that a sin promises us. Even though we know it is evil, we convince ourselves of an apparent good—a false good—in order to justify why we need to commit a particular sin. Sin thrives in confusion, emotional absorption, fallen pleasures, apparent goods, the intensity of particular moments, as well as flashy and fleshy false promises.

Sin runs a very popular campaign to convince the children of God that its promises are more rewarding, satisfying, and enjoyable than the promises of God. But these are all lies and such a campaign comes straight from Hell.

We also experience a similar inclination in neglecting to do good. We can ignore the good things to which we are called. We can lie to ourselves that we have given enough, or are not qualified enough to do some good, or convince ourselves that someone else can do it. In the face of a good act that we are summoned to do, we choose not to do it and allow something else to distract us or fill our time.

> Religion that is pure and undefiled before God, the Father, is this: to care for orphans and widows in their distress, and to keep oneself unstained by the world. — James 1:27

Traditionally, we make the distinction between sins of commission and sins of omission. *Commission* is the term used for the sins born from evil acts we do. *Omission* is the term used for the good acts we fail to do.

St. Paul himself struggled to do good and avoid evil. In this intense exchange within himself, the apostle almost surrenders to a sense of complete desolation, but then returns to the Lord Jesus and declares his trust in Him.

> I do not understand my own actions. For I do not do what I want, but I do the very thing I hate.... For I do not do the good I want, but the evil I do not want is what I do.... Wretched man that I am! Who will rescue me from this body of death? Thanks be to God through Jesus Christ our Lord! — Romans 7:15, 19, 24-25

In moments of temptation, whether to do evil or avoid good, we must recognize and renounce the lure of sin and reject its mastery over us. We must not allow sin to rule our hearts and have sway over our souls. In times of temptation, we must declare Jesus Christ as the Lord of our lives and choose only His most excellent way of love.

> Take care, brothers and sisters, that none of you may have an evil, unbelieving heart that turns away from the living God. But exhort one another every day, as long as it is called "today," so that none of you may be hardened by the deceitfulness of sin. For we have become partners of Christ, if only we hold our first confidence firm to the end. — Hebrews 3:12-14

In my discipleship, do I recognize the influence and the lure of evil in my heart? Do I name and reject its lies and refuse to be mastered by its deceptions?

Pornography and the Lure of Evil

Our fallen world is currently being flooded with pornography. What was once readily considered filth, is now permitted on public ads and in the home through television and digital platforms. Pornography is a regrettable example of the lure of evil. Many hearts know that it is evil. We do not objectify another human being, a child of God, made in the image of our common Father. And yet, the lure of evil is there and many fall victim to its advances.

> Live by the Spirit, I say, and do not gratify the desires of the flesh. — Galatians 5:16

A Journey to Mount Carmel

Years ago, while I was working with college-age young people, a young man shared with me that he had been addicted to pornography since he was in middle school. It started with his first cell phone. He was lured by flashy ads and had quick and easy access. He suffered from sleep deprivation because he stayed up late at night watching pornography for whole durations of time. He avoided his friends so that he could watch more pornography. He couldn't develop healthy relationships with young women since every girl he looked at, he compared to the women in the pornographic videos.

The young man shared with me that he could hardly control his thoughts. His life was full of lust, self-centeredness, and loneliness. He was a slave to pornography. It had mastery over him. This is the way of sin. Sometimes it's blatant—like pornography—other times it can be discreet, such as in those addicted to gossiping, lying, and slander. Sin wants to be king. It desires a mastery over the children of God.

In the course of receiving spiritual direction, Christian-based therapy, and developing wholesome friendships, the young man above began to set boundaries against occasions of sin. He fought against internally objectifying other people. He adjusted his use of electronics and spent more time with real people in edifying interactions. All of these efforts show the power we have received in Jesus Christ, and the strength we have to fight the lure of evil and so live in the freedom of God's children.

> Out of my distress I called on the LORD; the LORD answered me and set me in a broad place. —Psalm 118:5

In our discipleship, we must apply as much an effort as possible, and fight as best we can, to recognize where the lure of evil has made inroads into our hearts and labor and suffer to remove its mastery and influence from our lives.

Do we realize that God seeks to lead us out of darkness and into His own wonderful light? Are we committed to abandoning sin and all its allurements so as to freely love God and our neighbor?

The Moral Law and Freedom

Our battle with the lure of sin would be fruitless if we were not blessed with moral truth. In His infinite goodness, God has given us His moral law. It is a gift. It is a light to our hearts.

> Through your precepts I get understanding; therefore I hate every false way. Your word is a lamp to my feet and a light to my path. — Psalm 119:104–105

When we speak of God's law, we have to distinguish between the moral law and the ceremonial law. The ceremonial law of the Old Testament was fulfilled in the Body of the Lord Jesus. We are no longer bound by its precepts.

> For he is our peace; in his flesh he has made both groups into one and has broken down the dividing wall, that is, the hostility between us. He has abolished the law with its commandments and ordinances, that he might create in himself one new humanity in place of the two, thus making peace, and might reconcile both groups to God in one body through the cross, thus putting to death that hostility through it. — Ephesians 2:14–16

Beyond the ceremonial law, however, there is the moral law. This is God's perennial law. Even as the Lord Jesus fulfilled the moral law, the moral law is still binding on God's children, since it helps us to order our nature and prepare us for virtue and a life in the Spirit.

As the children of Adam and Eve, we were created with a good nature. Due to Original Sin, we have a fallen nature. As such, we have concupiscence, that disordered attraction to evil and sin.

With our fallen nature, we can deceptively create a law according to our own flesh. In this context, the expression *the flesh* means an inordinate desire for evil, and not necessarily a synonym for our body. When we succumb to a law of the flesh, such as pornography or gossiping or disrespecting authority, we can allow ourselves to be ruled by a false law and call good things evil and evil things good.

In such a situation, we need guidance and instruction. And so, God's moral law, which is principally contained in the Ten Commandments, is our pedagogue, our disciplinarian. The moral law shows us right from wrong. It directs us to live according to human nature, sound reason, and our vocation as the children of God. It guards us from the mastery of sin and prepares our souls for the workings of grace.

> Therefore the law was our disciplinarian until Christ came, so that we might be justified by faith. But now that faith has come, we are no longer subject to a disciplinarian, for in Christ Jesus you are all children of God through faith. —Galatians 3:24-26

Before we can begin to desire virtue, we have to allow God's law to teach us. As we allow God's law to instruct us, it prepares us for freedom.

Oftentimes, we want to see God's moral law and our freedom as opposites, but the moral law is actually in service to our freedom. The moral law frees us from the lure of sin, the fluidity of our emotions, the heat of desire, and the passing trends of our fallen world. The moral law and freedom mutually need each other. They help prepare our souls for the workings of grace and the flourishing of virtue. They strengthen us to see the false mastery of sin and to seek and pine for God and His loving rule over our hearts.

The moral law and our freedom help us to declare and to show with our lives that Jesus Christ is Lord and our only Master.

> Therefore God also highly exalted him and gave him the name that is above every name, so that at the name of Jesus every knee should bend, in heaven and on earth and under the earth, and every tongue should confess that Jesus Christ is Lord, to the glory of God the Father. —Philippians 2:9–11

Do we welcome the instruction of God's moral law? Do we revere it as a protection against the lure and mastery of sin? Have we declared Jesus as the Lord of our lives?

With Our Master on Mount Carmel

As we fight against the lure of evil, our hearts seek a place of rest. We cannot always be solely in the spiritual battle. As we declare "Jesus Christ is Lord," we seek to be with Him, share fellowship with Him, and learn from Him, as the only Master and Lord of our lives.

Throughout salvation history, Mount Carmel has been a place of rest between God and His people. The holy mountain has always been seen as a place of safety and refuge. It has served as a consolation to the downtrodden and a strength to the weary. We see a vibrant testimony to Mount Carmel throughout the Sacred Scriptures.

The prophet Isaiah uses the leaves of Carmel to show that God can suspend His blessings. The plush environment of Mount

A Journey to Mount Carmel

Carmel was seen as a sign of God's presence and bounty. If such leaves could wither, then anything was possible.

> The land mourns and languishes; Lebanon is confounded and withers away; Sharon is like a desert; and Bashan and Carmel shake off their leaves. — Isaiah 33:9

Similarly, the prophet Jeremiah highlights Mount Carmel as a place to pasture livestock. The prophet sees the mountain range as a place that reflects God's care and goodness to his people.

> I will restore Israel to its pasture, and it shall feed on Carmel and in Bashan, and on the hills of Ephraim and in Gilead its hunger shall be satisfied. — Jeremiah 50:19

Additionally, the prophets Nahum and Amos exalt in the fresh water of Mount Carmel and use it as a sign that God can do anything, even dry up the powers of Carmel.

> He rebukes the sea and makes it dry, and he dries up all the rivers; Bashan and Carmel wither, and the bloom of Lebanon fades. — Nahum 1:4

> And he said: "The LORD roars from Zion, and utters his voice from Jerusalem; the pastures of the shepherds wither, and the top of Carmel dries up. — Amos 1:2

Mount Carmel is filled with multiple caves across its range. The caves became a place of hiding for many throughout salvation history. For example, King David, while on the run from Saul, dwelled in the caves of Mount Carmel. He and his military protected the shepherds who lived there and tended their flocks along the mountain range.

> So David sent ten young men; and David said to the young men, "Go up to Carmel, and go to Nabal, and greet him in my name. Thus you shall salute him: 'Peace be to you, and peace be to your house, and peace be to all that you have.'" — 1 Samuel 25:5-6

Following the tradition of the great Elijah, the prophet Elisha lived in the caves of Mount Carmel and used them as the base of his prophetic ministry.

> So she set out, and came to the man of God at Mount Carmel. — 2 Kings 4:25a

In addition, the prophet Amos references the intricacies of the caves of Mount Carmel and uses them to illustrate that God could find His people anywhere.

> Though they hide themselves on the top of Carmel, from there I will search out and take them; and though they hide from my sight at the bottom of the sea, there I will command the sea-serpent, and it shall bite them. — Amos 9:3

As Christians, who are preparing to be invested in the scapular of Our Lady of Mount Carmel, we must foster a Mount Carmel in our own hearts. We must labor to form a place of rest and safety where we encounter and are able to have fellowship with the Lord Jesus. We need a place that nurtures our relationship with the Lord and allows us to grow in His grace. We need a spiritual Mount Carmel.

Our heart is called to be this Mount Carmel, with leaves, pastures, springs, caves, and all. Our heart, and all its parts and portions, are to be a resting place for God to dwell in us and for us to share union with Him.

> The heart is the dwelling-place where I am, where I live; according to the Semitic or Biblical expression, the heart is the place "to which I withdraw." The heart is our hidden center, beyond the grasp of our reason and of others; only the Spirit of God can fathom the human heart and know it fully. The heart of the place of decision, deeper than our psychic drives. It is the place of truth, where we choose life or death. It is the place of encounter, because as image of God we live in relation: it is the place of covenant. —*Catechism of the Catholic Church*, 2563

Do I work to develop a spiritual Mount Carmel in my own heart? Am I attentive to my time with the Lord Jesus and work to develop a stronger relationship with Him?

Mary, the First Disciple

As we seek to renounce the lure of evil and the mastery of sin and to live with Jesus Christ as the Lord and Master of our lives, we can turn to the Blessed Virgin Mary. Our Lady was her Son's first and most preeminent disciple. Mary knew, loved, and wholeheartedly served the Lord Jesus. There were no conditions, no hesitations, no denials.

The Lord Jesus attested to Our Lady's discipleship and spiritual closeness to Him during an encounter in the public ministry:

> While he was still speaking to the crowds, his mother and his brothers were standing outside, wanting to speak to him. Someone told him, "Look, your mother and your brothers are standing outside, wanting to speak to you." But to the one who had told him this, Jesus replied, "Who is my mother, and who are my brothers?" And pointing to his disciples, he said, "Here are my mother and my brothers! For whoever does the will of my Father in heaven is my brother and sister and mother." — Matthew 12:46-50

In the account, the Lord Jesus is not rejecting His Mother or kinsmen, rather He is broadening His family. He is praising Our Lady who "does the will of my Father in heaven." The Blessed Virgin Mary is the exemplar and the model of what it means to follow the Lord, to give the obedience of faith to Him, and to follow His most excellent way of love.

In our lives, do we turn to Mary as the First Disciple and seek her guidance and intercession? Do we imitate Our Lady in doing the will of our Father in Heaven?

Spiritual Exercises

After finishing the teachings for today, the following spiritual exercises are provided. The exercises are the heart of the daily preparation for the investiture in the Brown Scapular. Not all of these exercises must be done. They are provided as a small treasure chest for your spiritual preparation.

Examination of Conscience

This examination of conscience can help with your general moral awareness of what it means to follow the Lord Jesus. In addition, it is strongly recommended that you go to Confession during your time of preparation.

- Do I remain vigilant and watch for the influences of sin in my life?
- Have I nurtured the lure of sin in my own soul?
- Have I been attentive to what I look at or watch?
- Am I attentive to what I listen to or hear?
- Do I have a healthy suspicion of myself in time of temptation?
- Do I seek the guidance of moral truth in moments of confusion and uncertainty?
- Do I frequent the Sacrament of Confession for a sober assessment of myself?
- Do I guard the freedom of my heart from all attachment to sin?
- Do I protect those under my care from the lure of sin?
- Do I order the things of life so that Jesus is truly Lord of my heart?

Praying the Holy Mass

As the summit and source of the Christian way of life, reflect upon the Holy Mass. In particular, pray over the *Confiteor*: "I confess to almighty God and to you, my brothers and sisters, that I have greatly sinned in my thoughts and in my words, in what I have done, and in what I have failed to do; through my fault, through my fault, through my most grievous fault; therefore I ask blessed Mary ever-virgin, all the angels and saints, and you, my brothers and sisters, to pray for me to the Lord our God. Amen."

Consider: (1) the expression of heartfelt contrition, (2) the acknowledgment of sins of commission and omission, and (3) the request for prayers and the desire for reconciliation with God.

Marian Devotion: The Angelus

℣: The angel of the Lord declared unto Mary,
℟: And she conceived of the Holy Spirit.

Hail Mary, full of grace, the Lord is with you; blessed are you among women, and blessed is the fruit of your womb, Jesus. Holy Mary, Mother of God, pray for us sinners now and at the hour of our death. Amen.

℣: Behold the handmaid of the Lord,
℟: Be it done unto me according to your Word.
   Hail Mary ...

℣: And the Word was made flesh,
℟: And dwelt among us.
   Hail Mary ...

℣: Pray for us, O holy Mother of God,
℟: That we may be made worthy of the promises of Christ.

Let us pray. Pour forth, we beseech You, O Lord, Your grace into our hearts: that we, to whom the Incarnation of Christ Your Son was made known by the message of an angel, may by His Passion and Cross be brought to the glory of His Resurrection. Through the same Christ our Lord. Amen.

℣: Glory be to the Father, and the Son, and the Holy Spirit,
℟: As it was in the beginning, is now, and ever shall be, world without end. Amen.

Divine Wisdom: The Christian Virtues

Theological Virtues: faith, hope, and love
Cardinal Virtues: prudence, justice, temperance, fortitude

Three Optional Prayer Methods

1. Lectio Divina

Spend some time, perhaps even fifteen minutes, repeating and breathing into your heart the following portion of the living Word of God:

> Then the righteous will answer him, "Lord, when was it that we saw you hungry and gave you food, or thirsty and gave you something to drink? And when was it that we saw you a stranger and welcomed you, or naked and gave you clothing? And when was it that we saw you sick or in prison and visited you?" And the king will answer them, "Truly I tell you, just as you did it to one of the least of these who are members of my family, you did it to me." (Matt. 25:37–40)

Consider: The majestic Lord sitting on His glorious throne during your particular judgment at the end of your life. Reflect on how He will judge you, both by the sins of commission and omission. Evaluate where you stand in terms of the good that you are called to do, and the evil you are called to avoid. Ask for the grace to be prepared and ready for the Day of Judgment.

2. Composition of Place Meditation

Enter into a contemplation of place. Use your spiritual imagination and compose a place. Imagine the sights, smells, sounds, taste, and touch of the environment. Allow yourself to be truly, spiritually present in that moment.

Compose the scene of Zacchaeus, a short man with great power. Imagine his small, plumpish figure. See his fine robes, well-tailored and beautiful. See his fine belt and sandals. Smell the fine fragrance of the oil in his well-groomed hair and beard. Hear the jingling of the coins in his tax collector money bag. Hear also the whispered derogatory comments about him. Imagine how different he is compared to the poverty and suffering around him. Imagine him trying to see Jesus. Watch as he climbs a tree. Imagine the branches of the tree on his hands as he climbs. Watch as he sees the Lord. Look at the Lord with Zacchaeus. Open your heart to Him. Speak to Him. Declare Him your Lord. See Luke 19:1–10.

3. Poustinia Meditation

Unlike others methods of prayer, the task of the Poustinia Meditation *is to clear your mind of all thoughts and attempt to think of nothing other than a simple word or expression. We can remain quiet and wait for a word to be given to us, or we can select a word before our time of prayer. The word or expression, whether given or selected, is repeated multiple times or simply held in our minds. Sometimes the use of a foreign word can help us stay focused. For our exercise today, we can use* freedom, heart, *or* Master.

Suggested Saints and Holy Ones

As Christians, we are surrounded by "a cloud of witnesses"—the saints and holy ones in Heaven who intercede and help us. On this third day of our preparation, we can turn to St. Maximilian Kolbe. As a priest during World War II, he experienced widespread fear and the lure of evil to remain silent and not speak the truth. Many people chose to ignore evil and look the other way. Saint Maximilian Kolbe, however, refused the lure of sinful fear and silence. He openly preached the gospel and defended the weak and persecuted. Such boldness led to his arrest and imprisonment in the Auschwitz concentration camp. Saint Maximilian Kolbe even brought selfless service and hope into the camp, which was a Hell on earth. He died taking the place of another inmate who had been selected for summary execution after the man asked for pardon because he was a husband and father. In our lives, we are called to fight the lure of evil and all its lies and speak the truth in Jesus Christ, no matter the cost.

Stations of the Cross Suggestion

The Stations of the Cross are recommended. They can all be prayed or simply the Second Station: Jesus Accepts His Cross. Reflect on the power the Lord has given to you. Pray to use that power to avoid the lure of evil, even if it means carrying a cross. Ask for the grace to remain free from sin and to live always in the freedom of the children of God.

Rosary Suggestion

The Rosary is always recommended. Today, the Sorrowful Mysteries are suggested. In particular, the Third Mystery of the Scourging at the Pillar is proposed. Reflect on your spiritual battle against the lure of sin. Declare Jesus as the only Master of your life.

Three Traditional Prayers

Act of Contrition

> O my God, I am heartily sorry for having offended You, and I detest all my sins because of Your just punishments, but most of all, because they offend You, my God, Who are all-good and deserving of all my love. I firmly resolve,

with the help of Your grace, to sin no more and to avoid the near occasions of sin. Amen.

Prayer before an Image of Our Lady of Mount Carmel

O God, You have given us Mary as our Mother and through the Order of Carmel we learn to call her sister. May we imitate her goodness and faith, and be ever joyful in the wonderful things You have done for us. May Mary watch over and protect us on our pilgrim way to Your holy mountain, Christ the Lord. We make our prayer through the same Christ, our Lord. Amen.

Prayer of Fatima

O my Jesus, forgive us our sins, save us from the fires of Hell, and lead all souls into Heaven, especially those in most need of mercy. Amen.

Fourth Day

Renouncing Satan

*Discipline yourselves, keep
alert. Like a roaring lion
your adversary the devil
prowls around, looking
for someone to devour.*

—1 Peter 5:8

PREPARATION

As you start Day Four, these simple preparatory acts will help you get started and keep you focused.

Today's Spiritual Goal:

To understand my third baptismal promise: "Do you renounce Satan, the author and prince of sin?"

Opening Prayers

Come, Holy Spirit, fill the hearts of Your faithful. And kindle in them the fire of Your love. Send forth Your Spirit, and they shall be created. And You will renew the face of the earth.

Lord, by the light of the Holy Spirit You have taught the hearts of Your faithful. In the same Spirit, help us to relish what is right and always rejoice in Your consolation. We ask this through Christ our Lord. Amen.

We fly to your protection, O holy Mother of God. Despise not our petitions in our necessities, but deliver us always from all dangers, O glorious and blessed Virgin. Amen.

O Blessed Mother, as we prepare to be invested in your scapular, help us to avoid the traps of the Evil One and stay faithful to your beloved Son. We rely on you. Amen.

TEACHINGS

After completing the simple preparatory acts, these teachings are provided so that a deeper understanding of the Christian way of life can be given and a true preparation can be made for the investiture in the Brown Scapular.

Degrading God's Children

In our discipleship of the Lord Jesus, we can oftentimes forget that we have a strong spiritual enemy who utterly seeks our demise and damnation. Contemporary false enlightenment denies the existence of the Evil One, but we believers know that the Devil exists, that he hates us, and that he seeks to perpetually separate us from the God Who loves us.

The fallen angel Lucifer, called the Evil One, the Devil, and Satan, despises us. He is aware that the only way in which he can grieve the heart of God is to destroy us, His children. As such, the Evil One is on a kamikaze mission to destroy as many of God's children as possible before the End Times. It is a kamikaze mission because the Evil One knows he has already lost, but he has time before the battle concludes.

Some years ago, I participated in the "exorcist school" in Rome. I was being trained in my capacity as a moral theologian, so that I could advise Church leadership over whether a possible demonic activity is within the moral realm, since sometimes a person experiences demonic activity because of the presence of sin in their lives and is not actually having a formal demonic possession.

While at the school, I was able to meet and talk with several trained and highly experienced exorcists who have encountered and fought bad spirits. It was an eye-opening experience that helped me to understand the maneuvers and activities of the Evil One in a more pronounced way.

While speaking with some of the exorcists, they recounted to me that one of the things the Devil enjoys doing during the administration of exorcism is to make the person, a human being, get on all fours and walk around like an animal, barking like a dog, snorting like a pig, or mooing like a cow.

I was initially confused by the account and asked the exorcists why the Evil One would do such a thing. They answered that the Devil takes sick pleasure in such things because every human person is a child of God and made in His image. And so, to have a human being act like an animal is to degrade both a child of God and the image of God within them. The Devil relishes in watching a child of God—bearing God's image—being debased by acting like lower animals without spiritual souls.

Such a story displays the evil and awfulness of the works of the Devil. He is the father of degradation who yearns for our damnation.

In our discipleship, we must be aware of the dark presence of the Evil One and work against him and all his works. We are the well-beloved children of God. We bear the image of our Father in our hearts. Our Father desires union with us. He calls us to Himself in His Son, Jesus Christ. He sends the Holy Spirit to sanctify, protect, and bring forth His Kingdom in us and through us.

Do we acknowledge the existence of the Evil One and stay attentive to his works and lies in our world? Do we fight against his efforts to degrade us by sin and evil?

The Rebellion of Lucifer

The Sacred Scriptures help us to understand the existence and person of the Evil One. We are told that the angel Lucifer was "full of wisdom and perfect in beauty" (Ezek. 28:12). He rejected God's authority and rebelled against Him. Many other angels chose follow him. As a consequence, Lucifer and his minions were sent to Hell.

For … God did not spare the angels when they sinned, but cast them into hell and committed them to chains of deepest darkness to be kept until the judgment. — 2 Peter 2:4

His tail swept down a third of the stars of Heaven and threw them to the earth. Then the dragon stood before the woman who was about to bear a child, so that he might devour her child as soon as it was born.… And war broke out in heaven; Michael and his angels fought against the dragon. The dragon and his angels fought back, but they were defeated, and there was no longer any place for them in heaven. The great dragon was thrown down, that ancient serpent, who is called the Devil and Satan, the deceiver of the whole world — he was thrown down to the earth, and his angels were thrown down with him. — Revelation 12:4, 7–9

The sin of the fallen angels was a total rejection of God and a denial of His goodness to them.

Scripture speaks of a sin of these angels. This "fall" consists in the free choice of these created spirits, who radically and irrevocably *rejected* God and his reign. We find a reflection of that rebellion in the tempter's words to our first parents: "You will be like God." The devil "has sinned from the beginning"; he is "a liar and the father of lies." — *Catechism of the Catholic Church*, 392

In the biblical account, the word *serpent* can be deceptive. The word is oftentimes merely given as *snake*. The word *serpent*, however, is much broader and actually describes something far more sinister. In the book of Revelation, we are told:

> The great dragon was thrown down, that ancient serpent, who is called the Devil and Satan, the deceiver of the whole world—he was thrown down to the earth, and his angels were thrown down with him.—Revelation 12:9

The account given in Revelation seems to suggests that the "serpent" was actually some type of dragon-like creature. Although using figurative language, the account is significant since it describes the Evil One as a fierce beast and helps us to understand the terror and distress that our first parents must have experienced in his presence.

The account shows us the terrible creature that entered the Garden of Eden. It shows us the terrible presence and power of Lucifer, who still holds all of his powers as an angel.

> Behind the disobedient choice of our first parents lurks a seductive voice, opposed to God, which makes them fall into death out of envy. Scripture and the Church's Tradition see in this being a fallen angel, called "Satan" or the "devil." The Church teaches that Satan was at first a good angel, made by God: "The devil and the other demons were indeed created naturally good by God, but they became evil by their own doing."—*Catechism of the Catholic Church*, 391

In our discipleship, we face this same creature. The Devil is not a benign talking snake, or a weak whisperer of lies. He is an angelic person, who is dreadful to behold and horrifying to fight. Do we realize the dark weight that is wielded by the Evil One? Do we place our trust in the Lord Jesus and refuse to be overwhelmed by fear or anxiety when fighting the Devil?

"I Watched Satan Fall"

The Lord Jesus, the long-awaited Anointed Savior, declared His opposition to the Evil One. He saw the Evil One fall at the beginning of time. He knew the battle was already won, but the fate of the human family laid in the balance.

> The seventy returned with joy, saying, "Lord, in your name even the demons submit to us!" He said to them, "I watched Satan fall from heaven like a flash of lightning. See, I have given you authority to tread on snakes and scorpions, and over all the power of the enemy; and nothing will hurt you. Nevertheless, do not rejoice at this, that the spirits submit to you, but rejoice that your names are written in Heaven." —Luke 10:17-20

Throughout his ministry, the Lord entered into regular battle against the Devil and fought against his lies and empty promises.

> Peace I leave with you; my peace I give to you. I do not give to you as the world gives. Do not let your hearts be troubled, and do not let them be afraid. You heard me say to you, "I am going away, and I am coming to you." If you loved me, you would rejoice

> that I am going to the Father, because the Father is greater than I. And now I have told you this before it occurs, so that when it does occur, you may believe. I will no longer talk much with you, for the ruler of this world is coming. He has no power over me; but I do as the Father has commanded me, so that the world may know that I love the Father. Rise, let us be on our way. —John 14:27-31

It is no coincidence, therefore, that the public ministry of the Lord Jesus was marked by extensive encounters with bad spirits and frequent exorcisms. The full force of evil was at work against Him. And yet, the Lord Jesus—true God and true man—stayed the course. Throughout His earthly life, He prayed to the Father and kept an intimate union with Him, obeying the Father in His human nature and trusting in His love as He fulfilled His mission to redeem the human race.

> In the days of his flesh, Jesus offered up prayers and supplications, with loud cries and tears, to the one who was able to save him from death, and he was heard because of his reverent submission. Although he was a Son, he learned obedience through what he suffered; and having been made perfect, he became the source of eternal salvation for all who obey him, having been designated by God a high priest according to the order of Melchizedek. —Hebrews 5:7-10

The Lord's entire life was a living oblation of love to the Father in service to the redemption of humanity. In the Paschal Mystery, which is His Passion, Death, and Resurrection, the saving mission of the Lord Jesus was completely fulfilled. By the Paschal Mystery, the Devil is vanquished, the human heart is made free, and salvation is offered to all. The Paschal Mystery, therefore, is the definitive victory of good over evil, of God's redemption over the lies and manipulations of the Evil One in this life.

Do we acknowledge the authority of the Lord Jesus over the Evil One? Do we seek to live out the Paschal Mystery in our own lives?

The Early Carmelite Hermits

As Mount Carmel was revered throughout the Sacred Scriptures, so it has always been esteemed in the history of the Church. Early on, there were Christian hermits who felt the call to Carmel. They lived near the springs of the mountain range and sought solitude in the caves and grottoes of the holy mount. They held vigil against the Evil One and petitioned for the building up and holiness of the whole Church.

As we also see in the tradition of the Desert Fathers and throughout the monastic tradition, such hermits were the front guard against the wiles and wickedness of the Devil. As men and women who were committed to penance and intercession, they became great spiritual warriors, who fought against the Evil One and his efforts to confuse and mislead God's people. In their fasting and supplications, the early Carmelite hermits became a bastion of spiritual defense of the Church and a model for all Christians on how to fight against the Devil and persevere under the Lordship of Jesus Christ.

In our discipleship, are we vigilant in our battle against the Evil One? Do we fast and offer supplication for our good and the good of all the holy Church?

Mary, Queen and Conqueress

In the battle against the Evil One, no one is more despised or hated by the Devil than the Blessed Virgin Mary. She exemplifies everything that he was called to be, but failed to do. Our Lady is trusting, obedient, and docile. She is the handmaid of the Lord and knows that whatever God says is both good and trustworthy.

> Then Mary said, "Here am I, the servant of the Lord; let it be with me according to your word." — Luke 1:38

Lucifer is the opposite. He is an arrogant spirit, who neither trusts nor will obey.

Our Lady is also detested because, although a human being by nature and below the angelic nature, she excels beyond the angelic nature and all creation by grace. God has blessed Our Lady in a singular way. She is above all others, including Lucifer. Our Lady is rightly hailed as the Queen of Heaven, and so the Queen of Angels. Mary is Lucifer's queen and he abhors her for it.

Our Lady is also a great fighter for the Lord Jesus and His Kingdom. She is known to be as terrible as an army in battle array. There is no competition against her, since she is perfected and strengthened by the grace of God in her divine Son, Jesus Christ, and she mediates that grace to all God's children. Lucifer is no match for her. He is a puppy compared to Our Lady who is a lion alongside her Son, the Lion of Judah.

> Who is this that looks forth like the dawn, fair as the moon, bright as the sun, terrible as an army with banners?" — Song of Songs 6:10

Saint John describes the spiritual battle between Satan and Our Lady. He gives an account of Our Lady's beauty and authority. She is clothed with the sun, the moon is at her feet, and she bears twelve stars around her head.

A great portent appeared in heaven: a woman clothed with the sun, with the moon under her feet, and on her head a crown of twelve stars. She was pregnant and was crying out in birth pangs, in the agony of giving birth. Then another portent appeared in heaven: a great red dragon, with seven heads and ten horns, and seven diadems on his heads. His tail swept down a third of the stars of heaven and threw them to the earth. Then the dragon stood before the woman who was about to bear a child, so that he might devour her child as soon as it was born. And she gave birth to a son, a male child, who is to rule all the nations with a rod of iron. — Revelation 12:1–5

The Handmaid of the Lord is the Conqueress of the Evil One. The Devil knows it and he dwells in perpetual bitterness over it. He knows the authority given to Our Lady by the Lord Jesus. This is why the Evil One seeks to distract us and attempts to keep us away from the Mother of our Lord and such a powerful advocate.

In our discipleship, do we ask for the protection and advocacy of Our Lady? Do we let her teach us how to love and serve the Lord more faithfully and zealously?

Spiritual Exercises

After finishing the teachings for today, the following spiritual exercises are provided. The exercises are the heart of the daily preparation for the investiture in the Brown Scapular. Not all of these exercises must be done. They are provided as a small treasure chest for your spiritual preparation.

Examination of Conscience

This examination of conscience can help with your general moral awareness of what it means to follow the Lord Jesus. In addition, it is strongly recommended that you go to Confession during your time of preparation.

- Do I acknowledge the reality of the Devil and understand his dark presence in our world?
- Do I remain vigilant against the influence of the Evil One in my life?
- Do I avoid anything that will disparage the image of God within me?
- Do I regularly go to Confession?
- Do I fortify my soul by prayer and fasting?
- Do I accuse myself of pride and fight against it?
- Have I sought ways to humbly serve others?
- Do I offer supplication for those under my care?
- Do I avoid any act of idolatry, whether horoscopes, palm reading, or other such things?
- Have I removed myself from situations or evil places that lack the presence of God?

Praying the Holy Mass:

As the summit and source of the Christian way of life, reflect upon the Holy Mass. In particular, pray over the *Hanc Igitur* of the First Eucharistic Prayer (Roman Canon): "Therefore, Lord, we pray:

graciously accept this oblation of our service, that of your whole family; order our days in your peace, and command that we be delivered from eternal damnation and counted among the flock of those you have chosen."

Consider: (1) the reality of Hell and the work of the Evil One to damn the souls of God's children, (2) the petition to peace between ourselves and God, and (3) the desire and supplication to be chosen and saved in Jesus Christ.

Marian Devotion: The Litany of Loreto

Lord have mercy. Christ have mercy. Lord have mercy.

Christ hear us. Christ graciously hear us.

God, the Father of Heaven, *have mercy on us.*

God the Son, Redeemer of the world, *have mercy on us.*

God the Holy Spirit, *have mercy on us.*

Holy Trinity, one God, *have mercy on us.*

Holy Mary, *pray for us.*

Holy Mother of God, *pray for us.*

Holy Virgin of virgins, *pray for us.*

Mother of Christ, *pray for us.*

Mother of the Church, *pray for us.*

Mother of Mercy, *pray for us.*

Mother of divine grace, *pray for us.*

Mother of Hope, *pray for us.*

Mother most pure, *pray for us.*

Mother most chaste, *pray for us.*

Mother inviolate, *pray for us.*

Mother undefiled, *pray for us.*

Mother most amiable, *pray for us.*

Mother admirable, *pray for us.*

Mother of good counsel, *pray for us.*

A Journey to Mount Carmel

Mother of our Creator, *pray for us.*
Mother of our Savior, *pray for us.*
Virgin most prudent, *pray for us.*
Virgin most venerable, *pray for us.*
Virgin most renowned, *pray for us.*
Virgin most powerful, *pray for us.*
Virgin most merciful, *pray for us.*
Virgin most faithful, *pray for us.*
Mirror of justice, *pray for us.*
Seat of wisdom, *pray for us.*
Cause of our joy, *pray for us.*
Spiritual vessel, *pray for us.*
Vessel of honor, *pray for us.*
Singular vessel of devotion, *pray for us.*
Mystical rose, *pray for us.*
Tower of David, *pray for us.*
Tower if ivory, *pray for us.*
House of gold, *pray for us.*
Ark of the covenant, *pray for us.*
Gate of Heaven, *pray for us.*
Morning star, *pray for us.*
Health of the sick, *pray for us.*
Refuge of sinners, *pray for us.*
Solace of migrants, *pray for us.*
Comfort of the afflicted, *pray for us.*
Help of Christians, *pray for us.*
Queen of Angels, *pray for us.*
Queen of Patriarchs, *pray for us.*
Queen of Prophets, *pray for us.*
Queen of Apostles, *pray for us.*
Queen of Martyrs, *pray for us.*

Queen of Confessors, *pray for us.*

Queen of Virgins, *pray for us.*

Queen of all Saints, *pray for us.*

Queen conceived without Original Sin, *pray for us.*

Queen assumed into Heaven, *pray for us.*

Queen of the Most Holy Rosary, *pray for us.*

Queen of families, *pray for us.*

Queen of peace, *pray for us.*

Lamb of God, Who takes away the sins of the world, *spare us, O Lord.*

Lamb of God, Who takes away the sins of the world, *graciously hear us, O Lord.*

Lamb of God, Who takes away the sins of the world, *have mercy on us.*

Pray for us, O holy Mother of God. *That we may be made worthy of the promises of Christ.*

Let us pray. Grant, we beseech Thee, O Lord God, that we, Your servants, may enjoy perpetual health of mind and body; and by the glorious intercession of the Blessed Mary, ever Virgin, may be delivered from present sorrow, and obtain eternal joy. Through Christ our Lord. Amen.

Divine Wisdom: The Deadly Sins

Pride, greed, gluttony, lust, sloth, envy, and wrath.

Three Optional Prayer Methods

1. Lectio Divina

Spend some time, perhaps even fifteen minutes, repeating and breathing into your heart the following portion of the living Word of God: "Because your heart is proud and you have said, 'I am a god; I sit in the seat of the gods, in the heart of the seas,' yet you are but a mortal, and no god, though you compare your mind with the mind of a god" (Ezek. 28:2).

Consider: The rebuke of God to the Evil One, who was so blessed and endowed by God with such gifts and beauty. Reflect on the vile nature of pride. Evaluate your own pride and arrogance. Ask for the grace to fight against the Evil One and all forms of pride.

2. Composition of Place Meditation

Enter into a contemplation of place. Use your spiritual imagination and compose a place. Imagine the sights, smells, sounds, taste, and touch of the environment. Allow yourself to be truly, spiritually present in that moment.

Compose the scene of the Lord Jesus in the synagogue at Capernaum. See the simple wooden furniture of the synagogue. Notice the people coming into the place of worship, covering their heads and looking for places to sit. Smell the incense and oil of the holy place. Hear the jingling of the coins in His money bag. Hear the whisperings of neighbors saying hello and preparing for worship. Imagine worship begins. The Lord is teaching. He is loud and commanding. And then, hear the shriek of the demon. Watch the Lord's response. He silences the bad spirit. He raises His hand. He has authority. Open your heart to Him. Speak to Him. Declare Him your Lord. See Luke 4:31-37.

3. Poustinia Meditation

Unlike other methods of prayer, the task of the Poustinia Meditation *is to clear your mind of all thoughts and attempt to think of nothing other than a simple word or expression. We can remain quiet and wait for a word to be given to us, or we can select a word before our time of prayer. The word or expression, whether given or selected, is repeated multiple times or simply held in our minds. Sometimes the use of a foreign word can help us stay focused. For our exercise today, we can use* battle, victory, *or* salvation.

Suggested Saints and Holy Ones

As Christians, we are surrounded by "a cloud of witnesses"—the saints and holy ones in Heaven who intercede and help us. On this fourth day of our preparation, we can turn to St. Padre Pio. The saint was a Capuchin Franciscan who only wanted to love and serve God in obscurity. But God called him to be a great witness to our world and blessed him with abundant signs and wonders. Padre Pio could read hearts, bilocate, levitate, heal, and he bore the holy stigmata. The life of the simple friar was a living testimony to the power of God. And yet, such gifts provoked the Evil One. Padre Pio constantly fought the evil, both spiritually and physically. The Evil One wanted to cover Padre Pio with melancholy, self-pity, self-hatred, and doubt about God and the mystical gifts he received. Padre Pio, however, fought the good fight. He ousted the Devil and faithfully fought against him his entire life. In our lives, we may not have to physically fight the Devil, but we are called to resist the lies and temptations that the Evil One brings to the doors of our hearts.

Stations of the Cross Suggestion

The Stations of the Cross are recommended. They can all be prayed or simply the Ninth Station: Jesus Falls the Third Time. Consider the three falls of the Lord Jesus during His Passion. Reflect on your battles against the Evil One. Acknowledge that any fall along the way does not indicate an end of the journey. Ask for the grace to keep fighting the lies, false promises, and temptations of the Evil One.

A Journey to Mount Carmel

Rosary Suggestion

The Rosary is always recommended. Today, the Sorrowful Mysteries are suggested. In particular, the Fifth Mystery, the Lord Jesus Dies on the Cross, is proposed. Reflect on the victory of the Lord Jesus over the Evil One. Declare Jesus as the Lord of your life.

Three Traditional Prayers

Hail, Holy Queen

Hail, Holy Queen, Mother of Mercy, hail our life our sweetness and our hope. To you do we cry, poor banished children of Eve; to you do we send up our sighs, mourning and weeping in this valley of tears. Turn then most gracious advocate, your eyes of mercy towards us; and after this our exile, show unto us the blessed fruit of your womb, Jesus. O clement, O loving, O sweet Virgin Mary.

℣. Pray for us, O holy Mother of God.
℟. That we may be made worthy of the promises of Christ.

Let us pray: Protect Your servants, Lord, and keep us in peace. As we trust in the intercession of the Blessed Virgin Mary and all the saints, keep us safe from every danger and bring us to everlasting life through Christ our Lord. Amen.

Prayer to St. Michael the Archangel

St. Michael the Archangel, defend us in battle, be our protection against the wickedness and snares of the devil. May God rebuke him we humbly pray; and do thou, O prince of the heavenly host, by the power of God, cast into Hell Satan and all the evil spirits who prowl about the world seeking the ruin of souls. Amen.

Prayer for Peace

Lord, make me an instrument of your peace: where there is hatred, let me sow love; where there is injury, pardon; where there is doubt, faith; where there is despair, hope; where there is darkness, light; and where there is sadness, joy. O Divine Master, grant that I may not so much seek to be consoled, as to console; to be understood, as to understand; to be loved, as to love. For it is in giving that we receive, it is in pardoning that we are pardoned, and it is in dying that we are born to eternal life. Amen.

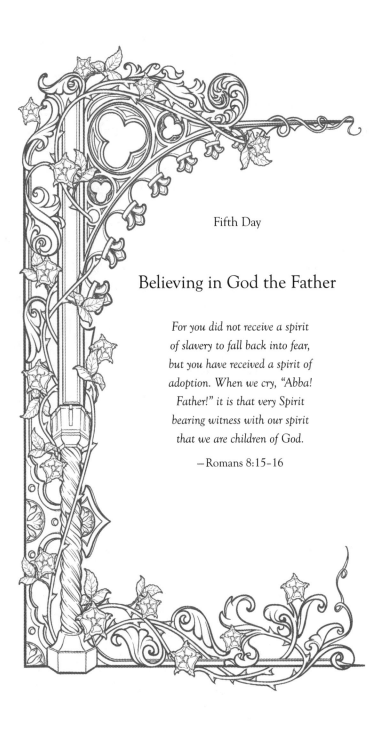

Fifth Day

Believing in God the Father

*For you did not receive a spirit
of slavery to fall back into fear,
but you have received a spirit of
adoption. When we cry, "Abba!
Father!" it is that very Spirit
bearing witness with our spirit
that we are children of God.*

—Romans 8:15–16

PREPARATION

As you start Day Five, these simple preparatory acts will help you get started and keep you focused.

Today's Spiritual Goal:

To understand my fourth baptismal promise: "Do you believe in God, the Father Almighty, Creator of Heaven and earth?

Opening Prayers

Come, Holy Spirit, fill the hearts of Your faithful. And kindle in them the fire of Your love. Send forth Your Spirit, and they shall be created. And You will renew the face of the earth.

Lord, by the light of the Holy Spirit You have taught the hearts of Your faithful. In the same Spirit, help us to relish what is right and always rejoice in Your consolation. We ask this through Christ our Lord. Amen.

We fly to your protection, O holy Mother of God. Despise not our petitions in our necessities, but deliver us always from all dangers, O glorious and blessed Virgin. Amen.

O Blessed Mother, as we prepare to be invested in your scapular, help us to love and believe in God our Father, through your beloved Son, Jesus Christ. We rely on you. Amen.

TEACHINGS

After completing the simple preparatory acts, these teachings are provided so that a deeper understanding of the Christian way of life can be given and a true preparation can be made for the investiture in the Brown Scapular.

My Father Owns the Store

There was a game show some time ago that had young people lined up at the entrance of a large department store. At a signaled time, the contestants were able to enter the store, but with a limited amount of time. The young people could run through the store and amass as many items as possible. They would be able to keep anything they collected, so long as they were able to get the items behind the finish line before the end of their allotted time.

As we can imagine, the contestants ran with fierceness, trying to pull two carts alongside them. They were grabbing things, throwing items, pushing merchandise, and sliding whole shelves into their carts. The time was ticking down. The crowd was going wild. The contestants looked stressed and overwhelmed as they scurried through the store and tried to grab as many things as possible. The entire experience was nerve-racking and traumatic.

On one episode, however, there was a young man who entered the store peacefully, casually walked down the aisles, and disinterestedly looked at the labels on some items. Such a response added more anxiety to the other contestants, as they perhaps wondered: "Why isn't he hurrying up?!"

As the time began to run down and all of the contestants made their way to the finish line, the peculiar contestant only had a few items in his hands. As the others were pulling along carts and dragging merchandise, they became aggravated by the other contestant. Finally, one of them threw down the things in her arms and yelled to the odd contestant, "What's wrong with you?! We only have a few minutes left! Why didn't you grab more things?! What's wrong with you?!"

The young man seemed shocked. He looked at his fellow contestant and replied calmly, "Oh, yes. Well, my father owns the store."

In our fallen world, we are told to hurry up, to push things forward, to grab what we can, and to believe and do whatever we want in order to get as much stuff and to achieve as much as possible. But our faith teaches us the liberating and peaceful truth, our Father owns the store. He is the Almighty One and the Creator of all things. The world is His and He shares it with us. The presence and the providence of God enlivens and imbues all things. We can be at peace, even as we have to make our way through the store of this life and fulfill our duties and responsibilities. We have the confidence of knowing that God is our Father. He owns the store.

> You are worthy, our Lord and God, to receive glory and honor and power, for you created all things, and by your will they existed and were created. —Revelation 4:11

In our lives, do we trust in God and rely on His goodness? Do we allow ourselves to have the peace and freedom of the children of God?

Fatherhood from Above

God is our eternal Father. He is all-powerful. He is the Creator of all things. He is Love. He is Mercy. God showers us with his tenderness and desires to show us to the goodness of his fatherhood.

The prophet Hosea describes the tenderness of God the Father:

> When Israel was a child, I loved him, and out of Egypt I called my son. The more I called them, the more they went from me; they kept sacrificing to the Baals, and offering incense to idols. Yet it was I who taught Ephraim to walk, I took them up in my arms; but they did not know that I healed them. I led them with cords of human kindness, with bands of love. I was to them like those who lift infants to their cheeks. I bent down to them and fed them.... How can I give you up, Ephraim? How can I hand you over, O Israel? How can I make you like Admah? How can I treat you like Zeboiim? My heart recoils within me; my compassion grows warm and tender. —Hosea 11:1-4, 8

Many people in our world today, however, believe that when we speak of God as Father we are only projecting our societal conventions and familial roles onto God. The argument is made that God is greater than any of our human titles and roles, and that by calling God *father* we have imposed our conventions upon Him. As a consequence, there are some who believe that it would be better for us to stop using what they perceive to be outdated familial structures and stop applying such things to God.

It is further argued by some people that the title and institution of fatherhood should be abandoned altogether, especially since so many people have been hurt or abused by their earthly fathers. In conclusion, it's believed that fatherhood is antiquated and is best left in the trash bin of the past.

Such worldly thoughts deprive us of an understanding of our heavenly Father and they miss some great biblical truths.

The Eternal God is forever *Father*. This is not a metaphor or symbol. It is not a title that we invented or that we impose upon

Him. God has always been and will always be *Father*. He has revealed Himself to us as Father. We are not forcing God into any human standard or social construct, rather God has disclosed fatherhood to us. Fatherhood is given to us from above, not imposed upon God from below.

From Adam to our present day, God has selected certain men to share in His own fatherhood. He has chosen particular men and strengthened them with the grace to live and exercise His own fatherhood in their respective families. As such, it is the human father Who has been given a divine gift, rather than the eternal God who is being forced into a human construct.

St. Paul tells us that every family receives its name from the heavens:

> For this reason I bow my knees before the Father, from whom every family in heaven and on earth takes its name. I pray that, according to the riches of his glory, he may grant that you may be strengthened in your inner being with power through his Spirit. — Ephesians 3:14-16

As every family received its name from Heaven, so every earthly father receives his fatherhood from our heavenly Father. The man is chosen by God and is blessed with the very Name of God, as his children call him *father*.

As such, it is essential to the sacredness of fatherhood that earthly fathers understand that they have been selected as witnesses to God our Father. They are called to live up to the high demands of such an esteemed vocation.

Do we revere fatherhood as a divine gift? Do we honor the men who are called to be fathers?

Fatherhood and Human Fallenness

Recognizing that fatherhood is a gift from above, we can soberly assess how such a gift is being fulfilled and lived out by the men who receive it. Human fathers are diverse. They are called from a wide spectrum of temperaments, personalities, abilities, and virtue. They have different backgrounds and personal histories. They have experienced different expressions of fatherhood themselves. From such a diversity, God bestows the gift of fatherhood. It is a weight of glory that is carried in the man's own fallen nature. As St. Paul teaches us, he holds such a treasure in earthen vessels.

> We have this treasure in clay jars, so that it may be made clear that this extraordinary power belongs to God and does not come from us. — 2 Corinthians 4:7

The gift of fatherhood is bestowed upon fallen men. Even the best of fathers will sometimes get distracted, make mistakes, and neglect the glory that has been given to them.

Unfortunately, and to the great suffering of their children, there are some fathers who willingly neglect or hurt their children. Some even abuse their own children. This is not the fulfillment of their vocation as fathers. This is a sacrilege against fatherhood itself.

As the children of such fathers grow up and are able to make distinctions, it is hoped that they may come to realize the difference between the gift and the sacrilege. Rather than the cause of spiritual distress, the truth of God's fatherhood and its authentic goodness and tenderness can be a source of healing and freedom for those who have been neglected, hurt, or abused by an earthly father.

God is our Father and He wants us to know the goodness and kindness of His loving fatherhood. He offers it to all and seeks to care for all His children.

Do I recognize the faults of earthly fathers and ask for healing from our heavenly Father? Do I allow God to be the standard of fatherhood in my life?

A Good Father

By exploring what is means to be a good earthly father, we see reflections of the fatherhood of God. By acknowledging good attributes of a father here on earth, we can better see and understand the face of our heavenly Father.

With this dual discernment in mind, we can turn to divine wisdom. The Sacred Scriptures provide extensive explanations and admonitions on what it means to be a good father. There many attributes that are expected of fathers, but divine wisdom summarizes them all and teaches that a father's love is expressed in how he protects, cares for, feeds, provides for, and teaches his children. These are the expectations of a good father. He is to fulfill each of them, and do so with virtue and a strong work ethic.

In His earthly ministry, the Lord Jesus describes a good father:

> Is there anyone among you who, if your child asks for bread, will give a stone? Or if the child asks for a fish, will give a snake? If you then, who are evil, know how to give good gifts to your children, how much more will your Father in heaven give good things to those who ask him! —Matthew 7:9–11

St. Paul uses the example of a good father to describe his apostolic ministry:

> As you know, we dealt with each one of you like a father with his children, urging and encouraging

> you and pleading that you lead a life worthy of God,
> who calls you into his own kingdom and glory. — 1
> Thessalonians 2:11-12

There are other sources in the Sacred Scriptures that develop the vocation of fatherhood:

The Bible teaches us that a father must always view his children as a blessing, especially in moments of anger or disappointment.

> Children, obey your parents in everything, for this
> is your acceptable duty in the Lord. Fathers, do not
> provoke your children, or they may lose heart. — Co-
> lossians 3:20-21

The Bible tells a father to be a model of virtue, especially justice and mercy.

> The righteous walk in integrity — happy are the chil-
> dren who follow them! — Proverbs 20:7

The Bible calls upon a father to be a man of virtue and to expect such virtue from his children. He is to hold his children to high standards, while providing the earthly and spiritual means for them to be successful. A father is to be tender, but also exercise discipline. He must be present and available when his children fail and need tough love or encouragement. A father's love must be constant and unconditional. He is to be a foundation for his children that never wavers or cracks.

> Children, obey your parents in the Lord, for this
> is right. "Honor your father and mother" — this is

> the first commandment with a promise: "so that it may be well with you and you may live long on the earth." And, fathers, do not provoke your children to anger, but bring them up in the discipline and instruction of the Lord. — Ephesians 6:1-4

A father dies to himself by loving his wife without deference to himself or his desires, as Christ loves the Church. In such a way, he teaches his children by word and example what it means to selflessly serve and redemptively suffer for another. A father's children witness his generous love to their mother, just as they also experience the same sacrificial love of their father towards them.

> Husbands, love your wives, just as Christ loved the church and gave himself up for her, in order to make her holy by cleansing her with the washing of water by the word, so as to present the church to himself in splendor, without a spot or wrinkle or anything of the kind — yes, so that she may be holy and without blemish. In the same way, husbands should love their wives as they do their own bodies. He who loves his wife loves himself. — Ephesians 5:25-28

According to the Bible, a father also teaches his children, especially his sons, about fortitude and charitable service to those in need, such as the widow, orphan, and other vulnerable people. A loving father understands that his paternal vocation is also to the common good of society, not solely his own family. Fathers are called to be attentive to the moves of culture and to defend the innocent and weak, especially children, from any possible aggressor or malicious influence.

These are some of the biblical points about being a good father. With each of the points, we are able to see more of the face of our heavenly Father. By exploring these biblical teachings, we are able to understand how much God our Father loves us, protects us, cares for us, feeds us, provides for us, and teaches us, His children.

Do we give thanks to God for His many acts of fatherhood? Do we cherish the attributes of a good father in the earthly fathers among us?

Elijah and the One, True God

After the division of King David's kingdom, the northern portion began to engage in widespread idolatry and moral evil. As a consequence, God allowed for a severe famine to strike the land. He also sent the prophet Elijah to the north to preach repentance and a return to the covenant and right worship. The prophet was known for his mighty works and fiery preaching. He was very close to the living God.

The prophet met the king of the northern kingdom and told him to assemble the priests of Baal and the prophets of Asherah on Mount Carmel. Knowing the authority of the prophet and the sacredness of Carmel, it was clear that such an assembly would be a showdown of some sort.

When everyone came together, Elijah asked that both he and the priests of Baal be given a bull for sacrifice. The wood for each would be set, but no fire would be started. Each was to call upon their respective deity and see which would light the sacrificial fire.

The four hundred and fifty priests of Baal moved forward.

> So they took the bull that was given them, prepared it, and called on the name of Baal from morning until noon, crying, "O Baal, answer us!" But there

was no voice, and no answer. They limped about the altar that they had made. — 1 Kings 18:26

In response, Elijah mocked them and called the people closer to himself. He made a trench around the altar and told the people to pour water over the wood three times. The water was so abundant that it filled the trenches around the altar. Then the prophet prayed.

At the time of the offering of the oblation, the prophet Elijah came near and said, "O LORD, God of Abraham, Isaac, and Israel, let it be known this day that you are God in Israel, that I am your servant, and that I have done all these things at your bidding. Answer me, O LORD, answer me, so that this people may know that you, O LORD, are God, and that you have turned their hearts back." — 1 Kings 18:36–37

At the prayer of the prophet, "the fire of the LORD" fell upon the altar and consumed the offering and dried up all the water in the trenches. When the people saw it, they fell on their faces and declared the God of Israel and the true God.

The account is as dramatic as it is suspenseful. The prophet Elijah on the holy mountain of Carmel shows the fire and power of God. The people, who were so seduced by idolatry and false views of God, were led to repentance and conversion.

In our own day, God continues to work signs and wonders. The work of the prophet continues today. Our task is to see the signs and to repent of our misunderstandings and misgivings about the living God. In spite of the fallen claims of some about fatherhood, we boldly declare God as our Father. Our further task is to accept the fatherhood of God and allow Him to mold and shape us so that we can be the prophetic instruments for Him in our day. We seek not simply to see the wonders of God, but to be the servants that He can use to further His work and Kingdom in our world.

Do we desire to have the confidence of Elijah and call God our Father? Do we recognize the signs and wonders of God today and seek to be willing instruments for Him and His Kingdom?

Mary of Mount Carmel

The early hermits lived lives of penance and contemplation. As they fought for the soul of the Church, they began to turn to the Blessed Virgin Mary. As Elijah was the spiritual father of all prophets, so they came to see Our Lady as the mother of all prophets. As they saw Elijah as the listener of God, so they came to a deeper awareness of Mary as the one who hears the Word of God and obeys it.

> But [Jesus] said, "Blessed rather are those who hear the word of God and obey it!"—Luke 11:28

In time, the early Carmelite hermits came to speak and pray to Mary of Mount Carmel. The first shared oratory of the group was dedicated to Our Lady. The hermits began to see their life on Mount Carmel as being lived under the mantle of Holy Mary.

In our lives, do we place our discipleship under the mantle of Our Lady? Like the early Carmelites, do we see her at the first and best disciple of the Lord and ask for her help and intercession?

A Journey to Mount Carmel

SPIRITUAL EXERCISES

After finishing the teachings for today, the following spiritual exercises are provided. The exercises are the heart of the daily preparation for the investiture in the Brown Scapular. Not all of these exercises must be done. They are provided as a small treasure chest for your spiritual preparation.

Examination of Conscience

This examination of conscience can help with your general moral awareness of what it means to follow the Lord Jesus. In addition, it is strongly recommended that you go to Confession during your time of preparation.

- Do I live as a child of the ever-living and all-powerful God, Creator of Heaven and earth?
- Do I praise Him for His paternity and kindness to me?
- Do I give public acknowledgment to His goodness to his me?
- Do I allow God to heal me?
- Have I shown reverence to the men among us who are called to be fathers?
- Do I honor my earthly father?
- Have I sought to imitate the attributes of a good father in my own vocation?
- If a father, do you put your wife and children first in all things?
- If a father, do you seek to protect, provide, and teach your children?
- Do I honor the spiritual fatherhood of the Church's leaders?

Praying the Holy Mass

As the summit and source of the Christian way of life, reflect upon the Holy Mass. In particular, pray over the beginning of the First Eucharistic Prayer (Roman Canon): "To you, therefore, most merciful Father, we make humble prayer and petition through Jesus Christ, your Son, our Lord: that you accept and bless these gifts, these offerings, these holy and unblemished sacrifices."

Consider: (1) the entire Eucharistic Prayer is addressed to God the Father, (2) the acknowledgment of the total mercy of God through Jesus Christ, and (3) the request that we be received and accepted by God the Father.

Marian Devotion: Acclamations in Honor of the Mother of Christ

Mary the Dawn—Christ the Perfect Day;
Mary the Gate—Christ the Heavenly Way!
Mary the Root—Christ the Mystic Vine;
Mary the Grape—Christ the Sacred Wine!
Mary the Stem—Christ the Rose, blood-red;
Mary the Wheat—Christ the Living Bread!
Mary the Fount—Christ the Cleansing Flood;
Mary the Cup—Christ the Saving Blood!
Mary the Temple—Christ the Temple's Lord;
Mary the Shrine—Christ the God adored!
Mary the Beacon—Christ the Heaven's Rest;
Mary the Mirror—Christ the Vision Blest!
Mary the Mother—Christ the Mother's Son;
By all things blessed while endless ages run!

Divine Wisdom: The Lord's Prayer

Seven Petitions:

- The first three relate to God: God's Name, God's Kingdom, God's will
- The last four relate to our neighbor: give us, forgive us, lead us, deliver us

Three Optional Prayer Methods

1. Lectio Divina

Spend some time, perhaps even fifteen minutes, repeating and breathing into your heart the following portion of the living Word of God: "Every generous act of giving, with every perfect gift, is from above, coming down from the Father of lights, with whom there is no variation or shadow due to change" (James 1:17).

Consider: The all-powerful God surrounded by light and glory. Reflect on the all-holy God being your heavenly Father. Consider the many good and perfect gifts which He pours down upon you. Evaluate where you stand and offer Him your praise and gratitude. Ask for the grace to be a faithful child of so loving a Father.

2. Composition of Place Meditation

Enter into a contemplation of place. Use your spiritual imagination and compose a place. Imagine the sights, smells, sounds, taste, and touch of the environment. Allow yourself to be truly, spiritually present in that moment.

Compose the scene of the return of the Prodigal Son. See the father, with his beard and sandals, watching the road and waiting for his son. See his sunburn and the wrinkles on his face, as he's waited day after day for the return of his boy. Smell the animals and mud that surrounds the old man as he's worked in the fields. Hear the prayers he utters quietly. Hear the sounds of the animals and the thumping of field equipment in the background. Now imagine his joy when he sees his son finally on the road. See his smile. Watch the tears roll down his face. Look at him run. He is near his son. Now place yourself in the young man's place. Feel the warmth of the embrace of your heavenly Father. Know His love and mercy. Open your heart to Him. Speak to Him. See Luke 15:11–32.

3. *Poustinia Meditation*

Unlike others methods of prayer, the task of the Poustinia Meditation *is to clear your mind of all thoughts and attempt to think of nothing other than a simple word or expression. We can remain quiet and wait for a word to be given to us, or we can select a word before our time of prayer. The word or expression, whether given or selected, is repeated multiple times or simply held in our minds. Sometimes the use of a foreign word can help us stay focused. For our exercise today, we can use* Father, sonship, *or* glory.

Suggested Saints and Holy Ones

As Christians, we are surrounded by "a cloud of witnesses" – the saints and holy ones in Heaven who intercede and help us. On this fourth day of our preparation, we can turn to St. Joseph. As the most-chaste spouse of Our Lady and the earthly father of our Lord, he was the head of the Holy Family. Although only a man, he was entrusted with the Anointed Savior and His Mother. He was called to be a true father to the Lord Jesus. He loved Him. He protected and cared for Him. He provided for and taught Him. St. Joseph is the best possible human reflection of our heavenly Father. In our lives, he is the best of models for every earthly and spiritual father. He is an inspiration to every parent and those who have the responsibility of caring for children and families.

Stations of the Cross Suggestion

The Stations of the Cross are recommended. They can all be prayed or simply the Fourth Station: Jesus Meets His Mother. Consider the closeness of mother and son, as He carries His cross. Pray for all families and parents today who are suffering and need consolation. Ask for the grace to trust and believe in God the Father in all situations.

A Journey to Mount Carmel

Rosary Suggestion

The Rosary is always recommended. Today, the Joyful Mysteries are suggested. In particular, the Third Mystery, the Lord Jesus Is Born in Bethlehem, is proposed. Reflect on the warmth and joy of the Holy Family under the headship of St. Joseph.

Three Traditional Prayers

Blessing of Fathers

God, our Father, bless these men, that they may find strength as fathers. Let the example of their faith and love shine forth. Grant that we, their sons and daughters, may honor them always with a spirit of profound respect. Amen.

Memorare

Remember, O most gracious Virgin Mary, that never was it known that anyone, who fled to your protection, implored your help, or sought your intercession, was left unaided. Inspired by this confidence, I fly to you, O Virgin of virgins my Mother. To you do I come, before you I stand, sinful and sorrowful. O Mother of the Word incarnate, despise not my petitions, but in your clemency, hear and answer me. Amen.

Prayer for Fathers

Heavenly Father, You entrusted Your Son Jesus, the child of Mary, to the care of Joseph, an earthly father. Bless all fathers as they care for their families. Give them strength and wisdom, tenderness and patience; support them in the work they have to do, protecting those who look to them, as we look to You for love and salvation, through Jesus Christ our rock and defender. Amen.

Sixth Day

Believing in God the Son

*Because if you confess with
your lips that Jesus is Lord
and believe in your heart
that God raised him from the
dead, you will be saved.*

—Romans 10:9

PREPARATION

As you start Day Six, these simple preparatory acts will help you get started and keep you focused.

Today's Spiritual Goal:

To understand my fourth baptismal promise: "Do you believe in Jesus Christ, his only Son, our Lord, who was born of the Virgin Mary, suffered death and was buried, rose again from the dead and is seated at the right hand of the Father?"

Opening Prayers

Come, Holy Spirit, fill the hearts of Your faithful. And kindle in them the fire of Your love. Send forth Your Spirit, and they shall be created. And You will renew the face of the earth.

Lord, by the light of the Holy Spirit You have taught the hearts of Your faithful. In the same Spirit, help us to relish what is right and always rejoice in Your consolation. We ask this through Christ our Lord. Amen.

We fly to your protection, O holy Mother of God. Despise not our petitions in our necessities, but deliver us always from all dangers, O glorious and blessed Virgin. Amen.

O Blessed Mother, as we prepare to be invested in your scapular, help us to love and believe in your divine Son, Jesus Christ. We rely on you. Amen.

Believing in God the Son

After completing the simple preparatory acts, these teachings are provided so that a deeper understanding of the Christian way of life can be given and a true preparation can be made for the investiture in the Brown Scapular.

"What if Jesus…"

Some years ago, I was attending an award ceremony and one of the guests of honor spoke with me about his adult son. The young man fought cancer and thought it was gone, but it aggressively returned with a terminal diagnosis. As his son went through the dying process, his father became his primary caregiver. The older man retired early, resigned from other commitments, and gave his whole life to his son as he lay dying.

While caring for his son, the older man told me he picked up the Bible and started reading the gospel books of the New Testament. Although he had been Catholic his entire life, and was now in his older age, he had never read the Gospel books in their entirety. Not only did he read them for himself, but he also read them aloud for his son. The father told me how shocked he and his son were by the demands of the Lord Jesus and how radical the way of life is that the Lord calls us to follow.

The older man continued and told me of a profound moment of conversion in his own heart, as a question spontaneously came to him, "What if Jesus really meant everything He said?"

As he cared for his son, the father told me that he found the real, in-the-trenches gospel message of Jesus Christ to be a source of strength and perseverance for himself and his son. He said he was ashamed of what the gospel was for him before his son's illness. He recounted how he previously wanted just jokes, cutesy stories, and warm fuzzies. He thought the gospel was supposed to be about his own emotional fulfillment and about feeling good.

Such a false gospel, however, did no justice to the life and teachings of Jesus Christ. And such a false gospel was no match for walking through the suffering and heartache of terminal cancer. It was only in the authentic gospel, with its challenges and calls to redemptive suffering, that any sense or meaning could be found in the throes of cancer.

In the light of such an awareness about the gospel, the father made a commitment to the Lord Jesus. He promised to live the gospel without compromise and to do everything the Lord asked of him as best he could. He decided to become a real disciple of the Lord. He would die to himself and seek to selflessly serve the Lord Jesus and his neighbor.

In the end, the man recounted that his son died a holy death. He was there with him as he took his last breath. As he told the story, the man chocked up with tears and said, "I would never have lived beyond my son's death if I hadn't read the Gospel and really came to know Who Jesus is."

The account of this father and son gives us a glimpse into what it means to believe in Jesus Christ and freely choose to follow Him. The way of the Lord Jesus is the Way of the Cross. It is the way of love that is willing to suffer for the good of others. It is the life of the Paschal Mystery, namely, a constant reliving of the Lord's Passion, Death, and Resurrection in our own lives.

Do we fully understand what it means to believe in the Lord Jesus? Are we willing to do whatever it takes to remain faithful to Him and follow Him wherever He leads us?

The Anointed Savior Comes to Us

The Messiah, the Christ, the long-awaited Anointed Savior comes to us. He is Jesus of Nazareth. He is God and man. No soul could have expected such an immense fulfillment of the ancient promise of a Savior. No heart could have anticipated such a rescue mission. The Anointed Savior is God Himself. God became a man and fulfilled His promise. He is our Savior.

> But when the fullness of time had come, God sent his Son, born of a woman, born under the law, in order to redeem those who were under the law, so that we might receive adoption as children. —Galatians 4:4-5

When the Son of God came, it was not as a removed figure falling from the skies. He did not oddly emerge from the sea, nor was He born from the mind of His divine father or from a peculiar sexual encounter, as was commonly said of divinities within the myths of Greece and Rome. The Son of God was not a ghost or a mere reflection of divinity. When He came, He came as one of us. The Lord Jesus did not come to us as an outsider, but as a human being, as someone within the human family. The Second Person of the Holy Trinity came as a human being! The divine Son became a fully human being and experienced all things truly human.

> And the Word became flesh and lived among us, and we have seen his glory, the glory as of a father's only son, full of grace and truth. —John 1:14

Humanity fell from grace when it turned away from its loving Creator. We were on a path away from the embrace of our heavenly Father, but the Lord Jesus freely chose to come and save us. He ransomed us from sin and conquered the kingdom of death and darkness. For those who turn to the Lord Jesus, sin has no power over them.

For God so loved the world that he gave his only Son, so that everyone who believes in him may not perish but may have eternal life. —John 3:16

The Lord Jesus removes our sin and shows us how to live as the children of God. As the Savior of humanity, and the source of reconciliation between God and man, Jesus Christ shows us the most excellent way of love. It is the way of salvation. It is the way to the Father's house. We could not fully know or follow it without the Lord. He reveals it to us and strengthens us by His grace to faithfully live and follow the way.

Holy Baptism

As Christians, we participate in the Paschal Mystery through Holy Baptism. The first of the sacraments is the means by which we share in the Passion, Death, and Resurrection of the Lord. As such, we should not diminish the primacy of our Baptism.

Not only does Baptism wash away Original Sin from our souls, but it also brings us into the New and Everlasting Covenant with God in Jesus Christ. God the Father adopts us, is well-pleased with us, and makes us members of His own family. We become temples of the Holy Spirit. Sin is removed at Baptism so that these greater, divine actions can occur within us. Baptism is truly our adoption ceremony into the life of the Holy Trinity—Father, Son, and Holy Spirit—and into the living household of faith.

The Baptismal Way of Life

As baptized Christians, we live as members of Christ's Body. As such, we relive the Paschal Mystery of the Lord every day in our lives. As the Lord Jesus died and rose again, so we are called to die to ourselves and so live for Him.

St. Paul juxtaposes two ways of life, and labels them as "life according to the flesh" (with *flesh* meaning our fallen attraction to evil and pleasure, and not necessarily our bodies), and "life according to the Spirit." In order for us to live in Christ and follow a life in the Spirit, we have to truly die to ourselves and our sinfulness, and seek to live according to the Person and teachings of the Lord Jesus.

> Do you not know that all of us who have been baptized into Christ Jesus were baptized into his death? Therefore we have been buried with him by baptism into death, so that, just as Christ was raised from the dead by the glory of the Father, so we too might walk in newness of life. — Romans 6:3–4

The Personal Decision for Jesus Christ

As we seek to understand our Baptism, we begin to deepen in our understanding of what it means to be a Christian. As such, we realize the importance of having an active and personal relationship with the Lord Jesus.

The grace of faith is poured into us at Baptism. In order for it to grow, faith requires a personal decision in our own hearts for Jesus Christ.

We have to intentionally choose Jesus as our Lord, Savior, and friend. Following the counsel of St. Paul, we have to "rekindle the gift of God" that we received in Baptism. We are called to live what we received in Baptism.

> From the outset, conversion is expressed in faith which is total and radical, and which neither limits

> nor hinders God's gift. At the same time, it gives rise to a dynamic and lifelong process which demands a continual turning away from "life according to the flesh" to "life according to the Spirit" (cf. Rom 8:3–13). Conversion means accepting, by a personal decision, the saving sovereignty of Christ and becoming his disciple. — Pope St. John Paul II, Encyclical *Redemptoris Missio* (December 7, 1990), 46

The Lord Jesus calls us to Himself. He looks upon us, pierces our hearts, and invites us to follow Him. Our summons is to rekindle the gift of God and to make a personal decision for the Lord. We declare that He is the fulfillment of all our hopes and dreams. He is the cause of our every joy. He is the only way to our salvation. We choose the Lord Jesus. We choose to follow His way, to love as He loved and to serve as He served. This is the beginning of a faith lived out. This is what it means to share in the Paschal Mystery and to be a disciple of the Lord Jesus.

We see the holy ones make this personal decision for Jesus Christ. St. Peter, our first pope, declared:

> Simon Peter answered, "You are the Messiah, the Son of the living God." — Matthew 16:16

In his encounter with the Risen Christ, St. Thomas made his personal decision for the Lord, when he exclaimed:

> Thomas answered him, "My Lord and my God!" — John 20:28

St. Paul made his personal decision for Jesus Christ as he announced:

> Therefore God also highly exalted him and gave him the name that is above every name, so that at the name of Jesus every knee should bend, in heaven and on earth and under the earth, and every tongue should confess that Jesus Christ is Lord, to the glory of God the Father. —Philippians 2:9-11

Have I made a personal decision for Jesus Christ? Have I fanned into flame the graces of God that I've received through Baptism?

The Mantle of Elijah and the Scapular

When Elijah, the Fire of God and father of prophets, was about to pass from this life, he was called to the Jordan River. He brought Elisha, his disciple, with him. As they reached the Jordan, Elijah struck the river with his mantle, and it parted.

> Then Elijah took his mantle and rolled it up, and struck the water; the water was parted to the one side and to the other, until the two of them crossed on dry ground. —2 Kings 2:8

After reaching the other side of the Jordan, Elijah asked Elisha what he could do for him since his life in this world was coming to an end. Elisha made the surprising and profound request for a "double share" of Elijah's spirit.

> When they had crossed, Elijah said to Elisha, "Tell me what I may do for you, before I am taken from

> you." Elisha said, "Please let me inherit a double
> share of your spirit." He responded, "You have
> asked a hard thing; yet, if you see me as I am being
> taken from you, it will be granted you; if not, it will
> not." —2 Kings 2:9–10

After the exchange, Elijah was taken from this world by a "chariot of fire and horses of fire" and the elder prophet "ascended in a whirlwind into heaven."

> As they continued walking and talking, a chariot of
> fire and horses of fire separated the two of them, and
> Elijah ascended in a whirlwind into heaven. Elisha
> kept watching and crying out, "Father, father! The
> chariots of Israel and its horsemen!" But when he
> could no longer see him, he grasped his own clothes
> and tore them in two pieces. —2 Kings 2:11–12

After the taking up of the great prophet, Elisha cried out and saw his spiritual father ascend to the heavens. Elisha cried out and once he could no longer see Elijah, he tore his clothes in sorrow. Elisha then picked up the mantle of Elijah and struck the Jordan, saying: "Where is the Lord, the God of Elijah?" The river divided again and Elisha was able to pass through the water.

> He picked up the mantle of Elijah that had fallen
> from him, and went back and stood on the bank
> of the Jordan. He took the mantle of Elijah that
> had fallen from him, and struck the water, saying,
> "Where is the LORD, the God of Elijah?" When he
> had struck the water, the water was parted to the

> one side and to the other, and Elisha went over. —2
> Kings 2:13-14

In the biblical account, we see the power of God manifested through the simple mantle of Elijah. The living God used the plain clothing of the great prophet to display His strength and goodness.

In a similar way, God blesses us through the Brown Scapular, which is an unembellished piece of cloth. God uses the scapular to bless and protect us. It was given to us by the Blessed Virgin Mary. It is a spiritual mantle of Elijah. It is the garment of the prophetic office. The scapular is a gift from God, a means by which we also receive a "double share" of Elijah's spirit.

Do I see the scapular as a gift from God, rather than as a piece of jewelry or a misplaced superstitious practice? Similar to Elijah's mantle, do I understand the power of God that works through the scapular?

Our Lady of the Resurrection

The Blessed Virgin Mary was present for the Paschal Mystery of her divine Son. St. John tells us that she was at the foot of the Cross.

> Meanwhile, standing near the cross of Jesus were his mother, and his mother's sister, Mary the wife of Clopas, and Mary Magdalene. —John 19:25

In terms of the Resurrection, we rely on Sacred Tradition, which tells us that the Risen Lord first appeared to His beloved Mother. While not mentioned in the written Gospels, the first appearance to the Blessed Virgin Mary explains why she was not among the group of women who went to the tomb at dawn.

> When the sabbath was over, Mary Magdalene, and
> Mary the mother of James, and Salome bought spices,
> so that they might go and anoint him. — Mark 16:1

These women had been the most faithful to the Lord during His Passion, and so were chosen to became some of the first witnesses to the Resurrection. If Our Lady—who held vigil at the Cross of her Son—had not already seen the Risen Christ, she would certainly have been in the group. Her absence from this group clearly indicates a previous encounter with her Risen Son.

Such a testimony from Sacred Tradition should not surprise us. The written Gospel books do not claim to contain an exhaustive account of the appearances of the Risen Lord. For example, St. Paul tells us that the Risen Christ appeared to more than five hundred believers at once. Such an appearance is not mentioned in the Gospel books.

> Then he appeared to more than five hundred brothers and sisters at one time, most of whom are still alive, though some have died. — 1 Corinthians 15:6

In this way, since the Blessed Virgin Mary was the first to see the Risen Lord, we can rightly call her Mary, Our Lady of the Resurrection. She is the Woman of prophecy and the mother of the Anointed Savior. She is Mary of the Paschal Mystery, Mary of the Resurrection.

Do I ask for Our Lady's help in understanding and living the Paschal Mystery? Do I ask for her assistance and intercession in following the Lord?

SPIRITUAL EXERCISES

After finishing the teachings for today, the following spiritual exercises are provided. The exercises are the heart of the daily preparation for the investiture in the Brown Scapular. Not all of these exercises must be done. They are provided as a small treasure chest for your spiritual preparation.

Examination of Conscience

This examination of conscience can help with your general moral awareness of what it means to follow the Lord Jesus. In addition, it is strongly recommended that you go to Confession during your time of preparation.

- Have I made a personal decision for Jesus Christ?
- Do I live with all the parts of my life under the Lordship of Jesus Christ?
- Do I give acknowledgment to Jesus Christ and speak openly of Him?
- Do I frequent the sacraments seeking God's grace in my life?
- Do I make acts of kindness to others?
- Do I generously show kindness to others?
- Have I sought ways in which I can present the gospel to those around me?
- Do I use my work as a way to give praise to God?
- Do I care for the spiritual health of those under my care?
- Do I seek the help of Our Lady in loving and serving the Lord?

Praying the Holy Mass

As the summit and source of the Christian way of life, reflect upon the Holy Mass. In particular, pray over the *Ecce, Agnus Dei:* "Behold the Lamb of God, behold him who takes away the sins of the world. Blessed are those called to the supper of the Lamb."

Consider: (1) the sacrificial love of the Lord Jesus for you, (2) the power of the Lord Jesus to remove all sin, and (3) the petition to be among His friends who are invited to be with Him and eat with Him.

Marian Devotion: The Regina Caeli

O Queen of Heaven, rejoice; Alleluia!
For He Whom thou didst merit to bear: Alleluia!
Has risen, as He said: Alleluia!
Pray for us to God: Alleluia!
℣. Rejoice and be glad, O Virgin Mary:
℟. For the Lord has risen indeed, Alleluia!

Let us pray: O God, Who through the Resurrection of Thy Son, our Lord, Jesus Christ, was pleased to give joy to the world, grant we beseech You, that like His mother, the Virgin Mary, we may obtain the joys of everlasting life. Amen.

Divine Wisdom: The Lord's Prayer

The Five Sermons of the Lord Jesus in St. Matthew's Gospel:
The Sermon on the Mount (Chapters 5–7)
The Mission Sermon (Chapter 10)
The Sermon of the Parables of the Kingdom (Chapter 13)
The Sermon on the Church (Chapter 18)
The Sermon on the End Times (Chapters 23–25)

Three Optional Prayer Methods

1. Lectio Divina

Spend some time, perhaps even fifteen minutes, repeating and breathing into your heart the following portion of the living Word of God: "and every tongue should confess that Jesus Christ is Lord, to the glory of God the Father" (Phil. 2:11)

Consider: the saving work of Jesus Christ and His offer of salvation to you. Confess His holy Name in your heart. Recommit yourself to the Lord with all your being. Reflect upon the glory of the Father. Ask for the grace to be a faithful friend and disciple of the Lord.

2. Composition of Place Meditation

Enter into a contemplation of place. Use your spiritual imagination and compose a place. Imagine the sights, smells, sounds, taste, and touch of the environment. Allow yourself to be truly, spiritually present in that moment.

Compose the scene of St. Thomas encountering the Risen Lord. See the Risen Christ, His shining countenance, His scarred but strong Body. See Him covered in robes of glory. Hear His peaceful voice. Smell the scent of roses, a reflection of His divine presence. Look at St. Thomas. The look of shock and embarrassment turning into faith and confidence. See the Risen Lord move His robes. Look upon the wound along His side. Consider the wounds throughout His Body. These are the wounds by which we are healed. See St. Thomas touch the side wound of our Lord. Feel the abundance of grace and faith flow into the room. Hear Thomas exclaim: "My Lord and my God." Look upon the Lord. Touch the wounds yourself. Declare Him your Lord and your God. Open your side and show your heart to Him. Speak to Him. See John 20:24-29.

3. Poustinia Meditation

Unlike others methods of prayer, the task of the Poustinia Meditation is to clear your mind of all thoughts and attempt to think of nothing other than a simple word or expression. We can remain quiet and wait for a word to be given to us, or we can select a word before our time of prayer. The word or expression, whether given or selected, is repeated multiple times or simply held in our minds. Sometimes the use of a foreign word can help us stay focused. For our exercise today, we can use Savior, Redeemer, or friend.

Suggested Saints and Holy Ones

As Christians, we are surrounded by "a cloud of witnesses"—the saints and holy ones in Heaven who intercede and help us. On this fourth day of our preparation, we can turn to Pope St. John Paul II. He was a disciple who loved the Lord Jesus and poured out his entire life in service to His Kingdom. He was considered a master catechist of our Faith and an evangelist of the highest order. He taught what he lived. He was a superb teacher because he was a faithful witness. The life of John Paul II was a life for Jesus Christ. There were no conditions or compromises. In our lives, we are called to imitate such powerful examples of our Faith and to live completely for Jesus Christ.

Stations of the Cross Suggestion

The Stations of the Cross are recommended. They can all be prayed or simply the Twelfth Station: Jesus Dies on the Cross. Consider the love that motivated such an oblation. Pray for the grace to follow the Lord on His way of love. Ask for the grace to trust and believe in the Lord Jesus.

Rosary Suggestion

The Rosary is always recommended. Today, the Glorious Mysteries are suggested. In particular, the First Mystery, the Lord Jesus Is Risen from the Dead, is proposed. Reflect upon the glory that has been won for us by the Passion, Death, and Resurrection of the Lord.

Three Traditional Prayers

Act of Hope

O my God, relying on Your infinite goodness and promises, I hope to obtain pardon of my sins, the help of Your grace and life everlasting, through the merits of Jesus Christ, my Lord and Redeemer. Amen.

Litany of Humility

O Jesus! meek and humble of heart, hear me.

From the desire of being esteemed, deliver me, O Jesus.

From the desire of being loved, deliver me, O Jesus.

From the desire of being extolled, deliver me, O Jesus.

From the desire of being honored, deliver me, O Jesus.

From the desire of being praised, deliver me, O Jesus.

From the desire of being preferred to others, deliver me, O Jesus.

From the desire of being consulted, deliver me, O Jesus.

From the desire of being approved, deliver me, O Jesus.

From the fear of being humiliated, deliver me, O Jesus.

From the fear of being despised, deliver me, O Jesus.

From the fear of suffering rebukes, deliver me, O Jesus.

From the fear of being calumniated, deliver me, O Jesus.

From the fear of being forgotten, deliver me, O Jesus.

From the fear of being ridiculed, deliver me, O Jesus.

From the fear of being wronged, deliver me, O Jesus.

From the fear of being suspected, deliver me, O Jesus.

That others may be loved more than I, Jesus, grant me the grace to desire it.

That others may be esteemed more than I, Jesus, grant me
the grace to desire it.

That, in the opinion of the world, others may increase and I
may decrease, Jesus, grant me the grace to desire it.

That others may be chosen and I set aside, Jesus, grant me
the grace to desire it.

That others may be praised and I unnoticed, Jesus, grant
me the grace to desire it.

That others may be preferred to me in everything, Jesus,
grant me the grace to desire it.

That others may become holier than I, provided that I
may become as holy as I should, Jesus, grant me the
grace to desire it.

"Jesus Prayer" of St. John Henry Newman

Dear Jesus, help me to spread Your fragrance everywhere I
go. Flood my soul with Your spirit and life. Penetrate and
possess my whole being so utterly, that my life may only
be a radiance of Yours. Shine through me, and be so in
me that every soul I come in contact with may feel Your
presence in my soul. Let them look up and see no longer
me but only Jesus! Stay with me and then I shall begin to
shine as You shine, so to shine as to be a light to others;
The light, O Jesus will be all from You; none of it will be
mine; It will be You shining on others through me. Amen.

Seventh Day

Believing in God the Holy Spirit

*And not only that, but we
also boast in our sufferings,
knowing that suffering produces
endurance, and endurance
produces character, and
character produces hope, and
hope does not disappoint
us, because God's love has
been poured into our hearts
through the Holy Spirit that
has been given to us.*

—Romans 5:3–5

PREPARATION

As you start Day Seven, these simple preparatory acts will help you get started and keep you focused.

Today's Spiritual Goal:

To understand my sixth baptismal promise: "Do you believe in the Holy Spirit, the holy Catholic church, the communion of saints, the forgiveness of sins, the resurrection of the body, and life everlasting?"

Opening Prayers

Come, Holy Spirit, fill the hearts of Your faithful. And kindle in them the fire of Your love. Send forth Your Spirit, and they shall be created. And You will renew the face of the earth.

Lord, by the light of the Holy Spirit You have taught the hearts of Your faithful. In the same Spirit, help us to relish what is right and always rejoice in Your consolation. We ask this through Christ our Lord. Amen.

We fly to your protection, O holy Mother of God. Despise not our petitions in our necessities, but deliver us always from all dangers, O glorious and blessed Virgin. Amen.

O Blessed Mother, as we prepare to be invested in your scapular, help us to trust and believe in the Holy Spirit. We rely on you. Amen.

After completing the simple preparatory acts, these teachings are provided so that a deeper understanding of the Christian way of life can be given and a true preparation can be made for the investiture in the Brown Scapular.

"The Holy Spirit Is Really Busy!"

Earlier in my priesthood, my ministry included serving as the chaplain of two Catholic high schools, the chaplain of several youth organizations, and frequent visits to the youth group of my parish. It's always a joy to be among the young Church. Their enthusiasm and zeal are contagious. Their transparency is a breath of fresh air. You never have to guess what they're thinking. Many times, the young Church says what older believers are thinking and feeling and it's a delight to see young people say it with such liveliness.

Case in point, on one occasion I was speaking with some young Christians and explaining the Holy Spirit and His work within our hearts and in the life of the Church. Like many believers, the young people didn't fully understand or realize how present and engaged the Holy Spirit is in our lives. In our conversation, I pointed out that we are fallen human beings. As such, we are not humble or noble enough on our own devices to turn to God and seek a relationship with Him. When we feel such a desire in our souls, it is the work of the Holy Spirit. God is initiating a relationship with us. We are only responding to His generous overture. Whenever we think, "I need to pray more," or "I need to go to Confession," or "I should reach out to that person in need," it is the Holy Spirit working within us.

Needless to say, the idea was earth-shattering to the young people. As one exclaimed, "Do you mean all those good things are the Holy Spirit?" "Yes," I replied, "He's always working to bring all of God's children into a closer relationship with Him." There was a pause and some serious reflection, when another young Christian broke the silence and responded, "Well, that means the Holy Spirit is really busy!" "Yes, amen," was my reply, as I felt a great smile cover my face.

The Holy Spirit is very busy. He seeks to bring us into a deeper living out of grace. The Holy Spirit is the life of the Church. He is the soul of the Communion of Saints. The Holy Spirit confects the absolution of sins. He will raise our bodies on the last day. The Holy Spirit is the one Who welcomes us into eternity. Yes, amen. The Holy Spirit is very busy.

Do I realize the presence and work of the Holy Spirit in my life? Do I readily obey His promptings and do whatever the Spirit asks of me?

The Holy Spirit

As God revealed Himself to humanity, we were shown that He is infinitely perfect and blessed in Himself and that He dwells as a communion of Persons: Father, Son, and Holy Spirit. Sometimes in our fallenness, we can think that God is a distant old man on a removed throne. But this is not how God has revealed Himself.

God has shown us that in His innermost essence He is not solitude, but family. God is a family of persons: Father, Son, and Holy Spirit. He is a Divine Family. The Father and the Son love and serve one another, and the love between them is the Holy Spirit.

God is three distinct Persons, equal in dignity and majesty, but united to one another by relationships of love. As such, the Holy Trinity does everything together. Each Person has a role to play in every action completed by the Godhead. This explains the important maxim: God the Father through Jesus Christ by the power of the Holy Spirit. In every action that God takes, there is an exchange between the Divine Persons, namely, God the Father acts, He acts through His Son, and always acts by the power of the Holy Spirit. One Person of the Holy Trinity never acts alone.

The Holy Spirit is the one Who brings the love and grace of God to humanity. He was sent by the Father and the Son and brings the saving work of Jesus Christ to the Church today. He confects every sacrament. He moves the heart of every person. He is always acting with the Father and the Son for our good, the good of all the holy Church, and for the entire human family.

> When the Advocate comes, whom I will send to you from the Father, the Spirit of truth who comes from the Father, he will testify on my behalf. — John 15:26

Do I recognize the workings of God — Father, Son, and Holy Spirit — in my life? Do I pray to the Holy Spirit and ask for the grace of God in everything I do?

The Holy Catholic Church

During the public ministry of the Lord Jesus, He founded His Church on the rock of St. Peter.

> And Jesus answered him, "Blessed are you, Simon son of Jonah! For flesh and blood has not revealed this to you, but my Father in heaven. And I tell you, you are Peter, and on this rock I will build my church, and the gates of Hades will not prevail against it. I will give you the keys of the kingdom of heaven, and whatever you bind on earth will be bound in heaven, and whatever you loose on earth will be loosed in heaven." — Matthew 16:17–19

There is one Spirit and one Body. The Church has continued in sacred continuity through the course of the ages. Through Holy Baptism and faith, we have become members of the Church.

> There is one body and one Spirit, just as you were called to the one hope of your calling, one Lord, one faith, one baptism, one God and Father of all, who is above all and through all and in all. —Ephesians 4:4–6

As we live out our relationship with the Lord Jesus, so we enter into a relationship with all other believers. No believer is alone. We are members of a community of faith.

As such, no one has an individual relationship with the Lord Jesus, in the sense that individual means an esoteric, "me and Jesus" rapport. Rather, believers have a personal relationship with the Lord Jesus in the midst of the Church, within the people to whom God is united by a covenant. There is no "me and Jesus," but rather a "we and Jesus" in the life of faith. It is important that we understand the difference between "individual" and "personal." My faith truly depends on others, and the faith of others depends on my faith. This is the mystery of the Church, born from God's covenant that was given to us in Jesus Christ.

> Faith is a personal act—the free response of the human person to the initiative of God who reveals himself. But faith is not an isolated act. No one can believe alone, just as no one can live alone. You have not given yourself faith as you have not given yourself life. The believer has received faith from others and should hand it on to others. Our love for Jesus and for our neighbor impels us to speak to

others about our faith. Each believer is thus a link in the great chain of believers. I cannot believe without being carried by the faith of others, and by my faith I help support others in the faith. — *Catechism of the Catholic Church*, 166

As we follow the Way of the Lord Jesus, we never walk alone. We are united to one another in the Church.

Do I see my faith in a communal way? Do I realize that the working out of my salvation depends on others, and that the working out of my neighbor's salvation depends on me?

The Communion of Saints

As we reflect upon our Baptism, we realize that we have been brought into the Divine Family with a vast communion of other people, made holy by Baptism and the workings of God's grace. We come to understand that all the baptized are reborn into a vocation of holiness and are truly *saints*. Grasping this divine truth, we begin to realize and see the living unity, the communion, among all the saints, all the holy ones, in Jesus Christ. Our vision is broadened by eternity and expanded by the realization of God's love. We come to see that our communion with other believers is not only to a specific, local community, or even with all believers who are alive throughout the world today. Our communion is with every baptized believer throughout the vast horizon of time and includes believers of every generation and place.

Not even death can break or diminish our communion with other believers. The Lord Jesus, the Risen One, has conquered death. The love of God, given to us by the Holy Spirit, is greater than death.

> No, in all these things we are more than conquerors through him who loved us. For I am convinced that neither death, nor life, nor angels, nor rulers, nor things present, nor things to come, nor powers, nor height, nor depth, nor anything else in all creation, will be able to separate us from the love of God in Christ Jesus our Lord. —Romans 8:37-39

At the time of death, a soul goes to either Heaven or Hell. We are still united to the souls in Hell, but they are lost forever. Some souls go through a process of purgation as they prepare to enter Heaven. We are obliged to pray and offer sacrifices for them as the Lord Jesus prepares them to see the Father. The souls in Heaven share in the glory of God. They are with Him and stand as "a cloud of witnesses" to us. They are the friends of God, and are our older brothers and sisters, who are still with us. They pray and intercede for us, befriend us, encourage us, and spur us on to victory in Jesus Christ.

> Therefore, since we are surrounded by so great a cloud of witnesses, let us also lay aside every weight and the sin that clings so closely, and let us run with perseverance the race that is set before us, looking to Jesus the pioneer and perfecter of our faith, who for the sake of the joy that was set before him endured the cross, disregarding its shame, and has taken his seat at the right hand of the throne of God. —Hebrews 12:1-2

As a baptized Christian, therefore, we belong to the communion—the family—of the baptized, the ones made holy by God's grace, both in this life and into eternity. No believer is alone. We are bound to one another by the love of God.

> I therefore, the prisoner in the Lord, beg you to lead a life worthy of the calling to which you have been called, with all humility and gentleness, with patience, bearing with one another in love, making every effort to maintain the unity of the Spirit in the bond of peace. — Ephesians 4:1–3

Do I turn to the saints often and ask for their encouragement and intercession? Do I pray for my fellow believers, those here on earth and those in Purgatory?

The Forgiveness of Sins

As the children of God, we share in the glory of our heavenly Father. As such, we can see the wickedness of sin, which diminishes who we are before God. Sin is a thief and a robber. It promises wonderful things, but only gives misery and alienation. As the children of God, we were not made for sin and our souls were not created for guilt. They do spiritual damage to us.

In light of this harm, the Lord Jesus instituted the Sacrament of Reconciliation, also popularly called Confession.

The Lord Jesus entrusted His apostles (and their successors) with the authority to absolve sin. As shepherds in His Name, the apostles, and their successors, the bishops—and the priests who have been given a share in this authority—continue the Lord's own saving work of removing sin, healing the broken, and restoring freedom to the children of God.

> Jesus came and stood among them and said, "Peace be with you." After he said this, he showed them his hands and his side. Then the disciples rejoiced when they saw the Lord. Jesus said to them again,

"Peace be with you. As the Father has sent me, so I send you." When he had said this, he breathed on them and said to them, "Receive the Holy Spirit. If you forgive the sins of any, they are forgiven them; if you retain the sins of any, they are retained." — John 20:19b-23

Do I regularly go to Confession? Do I understand the great gift the sacrament is to my discipleship?

Resurrection of the Body and Life Everlasting

By His Paschal Mystery, the Lord Jesus destroyed the Kingdom of sin and death. He is the Risen Lord and shares His everlasting life with those who love Him.

Jesus said to her, "I am the resurrection and the life. Those who believe in me, even though they die, will live." — John 11:25

In Baptism, we become the children of God by grace, and so heirs of the heavenly Kingdom. We share in the Lord's own Resurrection and glory. As such, death has no power over us.

It is that very Spirit bearing witness with our spirit that we are children of God, and if children, then heirs, heirs of God and joint heirs with Christ—if, in fact, we suffer with him so that we may also be glorified with him. — Romans 8:16-17

When we die in this world, our souls go for our particular judgment and we receive our eternal reward. Our bodies rest in the earth until the end of time. At the End Times during the Universal Judgement, our bodies will be raised and join our souls.

If we have loved God, cooperated with His grace, obeyed His teachings, and followed His way, then salvation will be ours in Jesus Christ. We will share in His eternal glory in Heaven. If we have refused to love God and follow His WWay, then we will dwell in Hell forever.

In our lives, we have to make the constant decision for Jesus Christ. We must allow His grace to transform us and strengthen us to love as the Lord loved and to serve as the Lord served.

Do I realize that a particular judgment awaits my soul upon death? Do I understand that I will give an accounting for the life I've lived?

Handkerchiefs, Aprons, and the Scapular

In the early Church, after the Resurrection and Ascension of the Lord Jesus, powerful miracles and displays of spiritual authority were poured upon the body of disciples.

> Now many signs and wonders were done among the people through the apostles. —Acts 5:12

God cured people through the very shadow of St. Peter.

> Yet more than ever believers were added to the Lord, great numbers of both men and women, so that they even carried out the sick into the streets, and laid them on cots and mats, in order that Peter's shadow might fall on some of them as he came by. —Acts 5:14-15

God further healed peopled through simple handkerchiefs and aprons that touched the body of St. Paul.

A Journey to Mount Carmel

> God did extraordinary miracles through Paul, so that when the handkerchiefs or aprons that had touched his skin were brought to the sick, their diseases left them, and the evil spirits came out of them. —Acts 19:11-12

In these healings, especially through the casual garments of handkerchiefs and aprons, we can see antecedents of the great gift of the Brown Scapular and the signs and wonders attached to it. In giving us the Brown Scapular, the Blessed Virgin Mary promised us her protection and blessing. In wearing the Brown Scapular, we are showing our consecration to the Lord Jesus through His Mother Mary, Mother of the Church, and Mother of Mount Carmel, with all its spiritual lessons and richness.

As we look upon the scapular, we are reminded and see a visible emblem of the work that God desires to do among His people. The scapular should not be taken lightly. God will use the simple cloth, as He used the simple cloths of handkerchiefs and aprons, to heal those who suffer and to manifest His presence and power in our world today.

Do I fully appreciate God's use of ordinary things to show His extraordinary goodness to us? Do I value the blessings and authority that have been given to the Brown Scapular?

Mary, Mother of the Church

Among all the followers of the Lord Jesus throughout time, both in Heaven and on earth, there is no one greater or who shines brighter than the Blessed Virgin Mary. She is the best and most preeminent of all disciples. As the Lord's Mother, she becomes our Mother. The Lord gifted her to us upon the Cross. Our Lady's physical motherhood was a gift given by God. He broadens and expands His gift and makes her the spiritual Mother of all believers. Our Lady takes this vocation seriously and approaches us a true Mother.

As our Mother, she counsels and directs us, as she did at the Wedding Feast of Cana when she told the servants and each of us:

> Do whatever he tells you. — John 2:5

Our Lady offers us her maternal warmth and kindness, so that we will draw closer to the Lord. She is always our advocate, constantly pointing us to her divine Son.

When praised by Elizabeth, Mary did not accept such praise, but turned the adulation to God. In this way, she models true discipleship for us and calls us to give all praise to the Lord Jesus.

> My soul magnifies the Lord, and my spirit rejoices in God my Savior. — Luke 1:46-47

In these ways, the Blessed Virgin Mary shows herself to be the Mother of faith. She is Mother of the Church, the Mother of every believer. She guides, advocates, and instructs us on how to follow the Lord Jesus. Our Lady loves humanity and perpetually directs us to her divine Son. She shows us the Lord's compassion and calls us to trust in Him. Mary is the handmaid of the Lord. She is a vessel of grace for humanity. Mary is our Mother.

Do I seek Mary's assistance and advocacy in my discipleship? Following Our Lady's counsel, do I seek to do whatever the Lord asks of me?

A Journey to Mount Carmel

SPIRITUAL EXERCISES

After finishing the teachings for today, the following spiritual exercises are provided. The exercises are the heart of the daily preparation for the investiture in the Brown Scapular. Not all of these exercises must be done. They are provided as a small treasure chest for your spiritual preparation.

Examination of Conscience

This examination of conscience can help with your general moral awareness of what it means to follow the Lord Jesus. In addition, it is strongly recommended that you go to Confession during your time of preparation.

- Do I acknowledge the presence of the Holy Spirit?
- Do I obey the promptings of the Holy Spirit?
- Do I pray often and ask for the guidance of the Spirit?
- Have I grieved the Holy Spirit by sin?
- Do I revere the Church as my Mother and teacher?
- Do I pray to the holy ones in Heaven?
- Do I pray for those in Purgatory and for those on earth who are in need?
- Do I regularly go to Confession?
- Do I show mercy to those who have hurt or offended me or a loved one?
- Do I show proper respect to the bodily remains of loved ones?

Praying the Holy Mass

As the summit and source of the Christian way of life, reflect upon the Holy Mass. In particular, pray over the Concluding Doxology and Great Amen: "Through him, and with him, and in him, O God, almighty Father, in the unity of the Holy Spirit, all glory and honor is your for ever and ever."

Consider: (1) the communion of the Father, Son, and Holy Spirit, (2) the shared work of the Holy Trinity in bring about our redemption, and (3) the union we have with Jesus Christ to pray through, with, and in Him.

Marian Devotion: The *Flos Carmeli* (Flower of Carmel)

Flower of Carmel, tall vine, blossom-laden;
splendor of Heaven, childbearing, yet maiden;
none equals thee.

Mother so tender, whom no man didst know,
on Carmel's children thy favors bestow;
Star of the Sea!

Strong stem of Jesse, who bore one bright flower,
be ever near us, and guard us each hour,
who serve thee here.

Purest of lilies, that flowers among thorns,
bring help to true hearts that in weakness turn
and trust in thee.

Strongest of armor, we trust in thy might,
under thy mantle, hard pressed in the fight,
we call to thee.

Our way, uncertain, surrounded by foes,
unfailing counsel you offer to those
who turn to thee.

O gentle Mother, who in Carmel reigns,
share with your servants that gladness you gained,
and now enjoy.

Hail, gate of Heaven, with glory now crowned,
bring us to safety, where thy Son is found,
true joy to see.

℣. Holy Mary, Mother of Christ, hear the cry of your servants.
℟. And bring down heavenly aid in answer to our prayer.

Let us pray: By a special privilege, Lord, You have adorned the
Carmelite Order with the name of your Mother, the most glorious
Virgin Mary. Grant as we faithfully remember this honor, that in
these days we may receive her protection and in the days to come
we may be brought to everlasting happiness. This we ask of You
Who are living and reigning forever. Amen.

Divine Wisdom: The Four Marks of the Church

One, holy, Catholic, and apostolic

Three Optional Prayer Methods

1. Lectio Divina

Spend some time, perhaps even fifteen minutes, repeating and
breathing into your heart the following portion of the living Word
of God: "And do not grieve the Holy Spirit of God, with which you
were marked with a seal for the day of redemption" (Eph. 4:30).

Consider: The presence and work of the Holy Spirit in your
heart. The call of the Spirit to grow in holiness and build up the
Church. Reflect upon the graces given to be an instrument of God
in His great work of redemption. Ask for the grace to be a docile
instrument of the Holy Spirit.

2. Composition of Place Meditation

Enter into a contemplation of place. Use your spiritual imagination
and compose a place. Imagine the sights, smells, sounds, taste, and

touch of the environment. Allow yourself to be truly, spiritually present in that moment.

Compose the scene of the Pentecost. Imagine the Upper Room, see its walls and floors. Smell the fire in the corner of the room and something being cooked. Hear the crackling of the wood in the fire. Look at the apostles, filled with fear anxiety. Watch them pace. Then feel the room shake. Hear the gushing of wind and crackling of thunder. Smell the fire. Watch the Spirit descend. Open your heart to Him. Speak to the Spirit. See Acts 2:1-13.

3. Poustinia Meditation

Unlike others methods of prayer, the task of the Poustinia Meditation is to clear your mind of all thoughts and attempt to think of nothing other than a simple word or expression. We can remain quiet and wait for a word to be given to us, or we can select a word before our time of prayer. The word or expression, whether given or selected, is repeated multiple times or simply held in our minds. Sometimes the use of a foreign word can help us stay focused. For our exercise today, we can use Spirit, Advocate, or communion.

Suggested Saints and Holy Ones

As Christians, we are surrounded by "a cloud of witnesses" — the saints and holy ones in heaven who intercede for and help us. On this fourth day of our preparation, we can turn to St. Teresa of Ávila. The holy woman is hailed as the "Doctor of Mystical Prayer." She was a great reformer in her day and called people back to the life of prayer. St. Teresa lived a life in the Spirit. She obeyed the promptings of the Spirit, even when there would be hardship and persecution. In all that she did, she sought to please the Lord and faithfully follow Him. In our lives, we are called to trust the Holy Spirit and obey His promptings.

Stations of the Cross Suggestion

The Stations of the Cross are recommended. They can all be prayed or simply the Fourteenth Station: Jesus Is Laid in the Tomb. Consider the resting of the Lord's Body as the Resurrection is imminent. Pray for the grace to experience the power of the Risen Christ in your own life. Ask for the grace to cling to the Risen Christ and to trust in Him throughout your life.

Rosary Suggestion

The Rosary is always recommended. Today, the Glorious Mysteries are suggested. In particular, the Third Mystery, the Descent of the Holy Spirit, is proposed. Reflect on the active presence of the Holy Spirit in your life and in the life of the Church.

Three Traditional Prayers

Prayer to the Holy Spirit

Breathe into me Holy Spirit, that all my thoughts may be holy. Move in me, Holy Spirit, that my work, too, may be holy. Attract my heart, Holy Spirit, that I may love only what is holy. Strengthen me, Holy Spirit, that I may defend all that is holy. Protect me, Holy Spirit, that I always may be holy.

Prayer of Pope Leo the Great against Worldliness

Grant to us, O Lord, not to mind earthly things, but rather to love heavenly things, that while all things around us pass away, we even now may hold fast those things which abide forever. Amen.

The Breastplate of St. Patrick

Christ be with me, Christ within me, Christ behind me, Christ before me, Christ beside me, Christ to win me, Christ to comfort and restore me. Christ beneath me, Christ above me, Christ in quiet, Christ in danger, Christ in hearts of all that love me, Christ in mouth of friend and stranger. Amen.

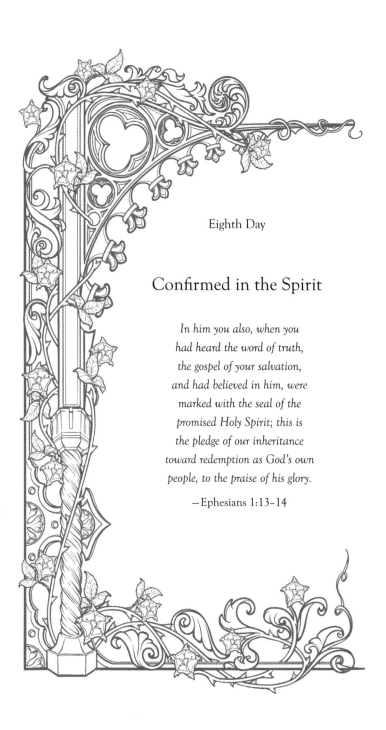

Eighth Day

Confirmed in the Spirit

*In him you also, when you
had heard the word of truth,
the gospel of your salvation,
and had believed in him, were
marked with the seal of the
promised Holy Spirit; this is
the pledge of our inheritance
toward redemption as God's own
people, to the praise of his glory.*

—Ephesians 1:13–14

Preparation

As you start Day Eight, these simple preparatory acts will help you get started and keep you focused.

Today's Spiritual Goal

To understand the formula of my Confirmation: "N., be sealed with the Gifts of the Holy Spirit."

Opening Prayers

Come, Holy Spirit, fill the hearts of Your faithful. And kindle in them the fire of Your love. Send forth Your Spirit, and they shall be created. And You will renew the face of the earth.

Lord, by the light of the Holy Spirit You have taught the hearts of Your faithful. In the same Spirit, help us to relish what is right and always rejoice in Your consolation. We ask this through Christ our Lord. Amen.

We fly to your protection, O holy Mother of God. Despise not our petitions in our necessities, but deliver us always from all dangers, O glorious and blessed Virgin. Amen.

O Blessed Mother, as we prepare to be invested in your scapular, help us to live in the life of the Spirit. We rely on you. Amen.

TEACHINGS

After completing the simple preparatory acts, these teachings are provided so that a deeper understanding of the Christian way of life can be given and a true preparation can be made for the investiture in the Brown Scapular.

Fully Initiated in Jesus Christ

The Sacrament of Confirmation is currently in a crucible in the life of the Church. In many places, droves of young people are confirmed, only to quickly make a mass exodus from the Church and the Way of the Lord Jesus.

Early in my priesthood, I chose to evaluate and explore ways in which we could lessen such a tide. In large part, observation teaches us that the single greatest response we can give is to guide young people to form a personal relationship with Jesus Christ. Nothing else compares. No program can compete with this simple, intensely biblical approach: form young people to know the Lord Jesus and teach them how to develop a relationship with Him.

If such a relationship is lacking, Confirmation makes no sense to the young person. They do not understand why they need this sacrament, and they don't realize what they receive through it. If such a relationship is present, then the young person yearns for the sacrament and readily seeks its graces of strength and vigor.

In this way, the important expression "fully initiated in Jesus Christ" takes on a new and deeper meaning. Young people understand what it means to prepare and wait for something, whether it's getting a driver's license or being selected for a sports team. As Confirmation is put this light, it helps young Christians to see its power and purpose in a clearer way.

As I would teach the young people, "In Confirmation, you become fully initiated in Jesus Christ. You're starting a new chapter in your discipleship with the Lord. You're now fully onboard and the Spirit wishes to give you greater strength to zealously live in the Lord and follow His Way."

It the Church today, it must be emphasized that Confirmation happens when baptized believers—who know and have chosen to live the Way of the Lord Jesus—freely approach and ask a bishop, as a successor of the apostles, to call down the Holy Spirit upon them. It is an act of freedom. It is an act of discipleship. Before the Spirit can be called down, however, the Christian has to renew their baptismal promises. This is an essential act since Confirmation "completes" Baptism and fully initiates a person into Jesus Christ.

In working to form young disciples, the emphasis on a personal relationship with Jesus Christ and being fully initiated in Him has proven immensely helpful.

Of course, such an approach is not only for young people. In our discipleship, at whatever age we might find ourselves, do we realize that the Holy Spirit has also been given to us? We have been fully initiated into Jesus Christ and are strengthened by the Holy Spirit to love and follow Him.

The Spirit has descended upon us to fortify us in our relationship with the Lord Jesus and His Church. Do we seek to fan into flame the gift we have received? Do we claim the graces of our Confirmation and seek to use them to grow in our own discipleship?

"We Have Never Even Heard ..."

In Acts of the Apostles, we hear about St. Paul's visit with the early Christians in Ephesus. After St. Paul spent some time with them, he realized that something was missing. He asked the Ephesians:

> "Did you receive the Holy Spirit when you became believers?" They replied, "No, we have not even heard that there is a Holy Spirit." Acts 19:2

Perhaps many people today might repeat the sad admission of the Ephesians and acknowledge that they do not know the Holy Spirit. This could be in part because the Holy Spirit does not speak of Himself, as the Lord Jesus taught us:

> When the Spirit of truth comes, he will guide you into all the truth; for he will not speak on his own, but will speak whatever he hears, and he will declare to you the things that are to come. —John 16:13

Although knowledge of the Holy Spirit might also be lacking because of a widespread neglect in preaching and teaching about Him.

As Christian believers, it's important for us to know the Person and work of God the Holy Spirit. Will we make this a priority in our discipleship? Will we discern the promptings of the Spirit and obey Him?

The Workings of the Holy Spirit

In our lives, it is the Holy Spirit—the Third Person of the Holy Trinity and the love between the Father and the Son—Who constantly moves in our hearts. He summons us to fellowship with the one, true God. He calls us to divine sonship and shows us the face of our heavenly Father.

> And because you are children, God has sent the Spirit of his Son into our hearts, crying, "Abba! Father!" —Galatians 4:6

The Holy Spirit also fulfills the saving work of our Redeemer. He takes the merits of our Lord's Paschal Mystery and applies them to our own hearts and to the entire Church today.

> Nevertheless I tell you the truth: it is to your advantage that I go away, for if I do not go away, the Advocate will not come to you; but if I go, I will send him to you. And when he comes, he will prove the world wrong about sin and righteousness and judgment. —John 16:7-8

In His sanctifying work, the Holy Spirit moves where His divine action is needed. There is no controlling His divine activity. The Lord Jesus references this movement of the Holy Spirit as He tells us:

> The wind blows where it chooses, and you hear the sound of it, but you do not know where it comes from or where it goes. So it is with everyone who is born of the Spirit. —John 3:8

As the children of God, therefore, we are called to have confidence in the Holy Spirit. We must look for His presence and seek His help. In joyful and difficult moments, the Spirit is with us. In times when we do not understand or when we struggle with the ways of God, the Spirit is present to teach us and lead us into understanding and prayer.

> Likewise the Spirit helps us in our weakness; for we do not know how to pray as we ought, but that very Spirit intercedes with sighs too deep for words. And God, who searches the heart, knows what is the mind

> of the Spirit, because the Spirit intercedes for the saints
> according to the will of God. —Romans 8:26-27

In my life, do I welcome the guidance of the Holy Spirit? In
hard times, do I turn to Him and seek His divine assistance?

The Spirit and the Lord Jesus

In our discipleship, the Holy Spirit is the one Who helps us to
make and live a personal decision for Jesus Christ. The Holy Spirit
works within us, therefore, to recognize and cooperate with God's
love. We need the promptings and inspirations of the Spirit. He
helps us to follow the Lord Jesus as His friend and disciple.

> Therefore I want you to understand that no one
> speaking by the Spirit of God ever says "Let Jesus be
> cursed!" and no one can say "Jesus is Lord" except
> by the Holy Spirit. —1 Corinthians 12:3

Have I made a personal decision for Jesus Christ? Do I allow
the Spirit to guide and direct me in my discipleship?

The Gifts and Fruits of the Spirit

As we listen to the Holy Spirit and obey His promptings and inspirations, we grow in the life of God. At our Confirmation, the
Holy Spirit blesses us with His seven gifts. These gifts help us to
grow in the supernatural life and to build up the Body of Christ.

> A shoot shall come out from the stump of Jesse,
> and a branch shall grow out of his roots. The spirit
> of the LORD shall rest on him, the spirit of wisdom
> and understanding, the spirit of counsel and might,

> the spirit of knowledge and the fear of the LORD.
> —Isaiah 11:1-2

As we cooperate with the gifts of the Holy Spirit and follow the way of the Lord Jesus, we begin to bear the fruits of God's Spirit. The bearing of the fruits of God's Spirit are a sign of His presence within us. They indicate to us that we are living the way of life God has called us to live.

> By contrast, the fruit of the Spirit is love, joy, peace, patience, kindness, generosity, faithfulness, gentleness, and self-control. There is no law against such things. And those who belong to Christ Jesus have crucified the flesh with its passions and desires. If we live by the Spirit, let us also be guided by the Spirit. —Galatians 5:22-25

By nurturing the gifts of the Spirit and flourishing in the fruits of the Spirit, therefore, we deepen in our discipleship and begin to reach a full stature in Jesus Christ.

> The gifts he gave were that some would be apostles, some prophets, some evangelists, some pastors and teachers, to equip the saints for the work of ministry, for building up the body of Christ, until all of us come to the unity of the faith and of the knowledge of the Son of God, to maturity, to the measure of the full stature of Christ. —Ephesians 4:11-13

Do I value the seven gifts of the Spirit in my life? Do I seek to bear the fruits of God's Spirit in everything I do?

The Carmelites and the Mendicant Charism

The Holy Spirit moves where He wills. He cannot be controlled or calculated. Such a reality can be seen in the life of the early hermits of Mount Carmel.

After the Crusades, many former Crusaders and pilgrims from Europe joined the ranks of the hermits. In time, many of these Carmelites felt a call to return to their homelands and bring the spirit of Carmel to the broader Church. As the Carmelites traveled home, they formed small communities in Cyprus, France, England, and other countries.

It was a movement of the Holy Spirit that summoned the Carmelites to leave the physical Mount Carmel so that the spirituality and charism of Carmel could be shared and nurtured throughout the universal Church. In this new phase of mobility, the Carmelites discerned the new and growing "mendicant charism" within the Church. Such a charism was made popular by the followers of St. Francis (the Franciscans) and the followers of St. Dominic (the Dominicans).

The word *mendicant* means "beggar," and the new charism called Religious to leave enclosed monasteries and to live itinerant lives, preaching and begging in the Name of the Lord Jesus.

The Carmelites recognized in this new charism a spiritual identity and help to their own mission of evangelization and spirituality. As such, the Carmelites became mendicant friars and traveled wherever they were needed, seeking to serve the Church and share the spirit of Carmel.

One such Carmelite friar was St. Simon Stock. It was to this noble instrument that Our Lady entrusted the Brown Scapular.

Such a history illustrates what it means to live in the Spirit and to follow His promptings.

In our lives, do we discern the will and workings of the Spirit? Are we willing to be uncomfortable and leave what we know in order to obey the Spirit?

Mary, Spouse of the Spirit

In the Tradition of the Church, Our Lady is hailed as the Spouse of the Spirit. The title is given since the entire life of Mary is surrounded by the presence and work of the Holy Spirit. In particular, Our Lady and the Holy Spirit cooperated together to bring forth the Incarnation of God and continued to cooperate together to build up the Church and bring God's grace to all humanity.

> Mary said to the angel, "How can this be, since I am a virgin?" The angel said to her, "The Holy Spirit will come upon you, and the power of the Most High will overshadow you; therefore the child to be born will be holy; he will be called Son of God." —Luke 1:34-35

In addition to working together at the Incarnation and throughout the Lord's public ministry, the Holy Spirit fell upon Our Lady with the apostles in the Upper Room. While her gift of the Holy Spirit was different from that of the apostles, it was a gift of great proportions. Our Lady cooperated with the Holy Spirit in being a Mother to the apostles and so assisted in building up the early Church and helping it to flourish.

> All these were constantly devoting themselves to prayer, together with certain women, including Mary the mother of Jesus, as well as his brothers. —Acts 1:14

> When the day of Pentecost had come, they were all together in one place. And suddenly from heaven there came a sound like the rush of a violent wind, and it filled the entire house where they were sitting. Divided tongues, as of fire, appeared among them, and a tongue rested on each of them. All of them were filled with the Holy Spirit and began to speak in other languages, as the Spirit gave them ability. — Acts 2:1-4

Our Lady continues to work with the Holy Spirit in sharing the good news of her Son and dispersing His grace upon all people. This is why we see Our Lady visit humanity and make several apparitions at different times throughout the world, whether at Guadalupe, Lourdes, Fatima, Knock, Akita, Kibeho, and many other places. In each of these visits, Our Lady is cooperating with the Holy Spirit and seeking to assist the Church and expand the Kingdom of her Son.

Do I realize the cooperation of Our Lady and the Holy Spirit? Do I turn to Mary and ask her assistance in obeying the promptings of the Holy Spirit?

SPIRITUAL EXERCISES

After finishing the teachings for today, the following spiritual exercises are provided. The exercises are the heart of the daily preparation for the investiture in the Brown Scapular. Not all of these exercises must be done. They are provided as a small treasure chest for your spiritual preparation.

Examination of Conscience

This examination of conscience can help with your general moral awareness of what it means to follow the Lord Jesus. In addition, it is strongly recommended that you go to Confession during your time of preparation.

+ Do I discern the promptings and inspirations of the Holy Spirit?
+ Do I seek to walk always in the life of the Spirit?
+ Do I seek divine wisdom in trying to understand God's will?
+ Have I petitioned for understanding to show compassion to others?
+ Do I seek the gift of counsel to know the hearts of others?
+ Do I pray for fortitude to remain strong in the Way of the Lord?
+ Do I pray for knowledge to fulfill my duties and responsibilities?
+ Do I fear the Lord in humble gratitude and thanksgiving?
+ Do I seek the intercession and spiritual motherhood of Mary?
+ Do I speak openly of God in public and among my friends?

Praying the Holy Mass

As the summit and source of the Christian way of life, reflect upon the Holy Mass. In particular, pray over the *Epiclesis* of the

First Eucharistic Prayer (Roman Canon): "Be pleased, O God, we pray, to bless, acknowledge, and approve this offering in every respect; make it spiritual and acceptable, so that it may become for us the Body and Blood of your most beloved Son, our Lord Jesus Christ."

Consider: 1) the invocation of the Holy Spirit during the Holy Sacrifice of the Mass, 2) the power of the Spirit to change bread and wine into the Body and Blood of Jesus Christ, and 3) the desire of the Holy Spirit to transform us and make us holy.

Marian Devotion: "Our Guiding Star" by St. Bernard

When the storm of temptation arises,
when you are amidst the reefs and shoals of tribulation,
fix your gaze on the Star of the Sea.
Call upon Mary.

Do the billows of anger, of avarice, of lust
batter against your soul—invoke her name.
In perils and sorrows and fears
fix your gaze on the Star of the Sea.
Call upon Mary.

Under her protection, you shall know no fear.
Under her guidance, you shall not falter.
Under her patronage, you shall reach your goal.
Fix your gaze on the Star of the Sea.
Call upon Mary.

Divine Wisdom: The Fruits of the Spirit

Charity, joy, peace, patience, kindness, goodness, generosity, gentleness, faithfulness, modesty, self-control, and chastity

Three Optional Prayer Methods

1. Lectio Divina

Spend some time, perhaps even fifteen minutes, repeating and breathing into your heart the following portion of the living Word of God: "And do not grieve the Holy Spirit of God, with which you were marked with a seal for the day of redemption" (Eph. 4:30).

Consider: the presence and work of the Holy Spirit in your heart. The call of the Spirit to grow in holiness and build up the Church. Reflect upon the graces given to be an instrument of God in His great work of redemption. Ask for the grace to be a docile instrument of the Holy Spirit.

2. Composition of Place Meditation

Enter into a contemplation of place. Use your spiritual imagination and compose a place. Imagine the sights, smells, sounds, taste, and touch of the environment. Allow yourself to be truly, spiritually present in that moment.

Compose the scene of the apostles Peter and John calling down the Holy Spirit upon believers. See their robes and dusty feet. Look at their bearded faces and smiles. Hear the rumble of the small crowd that's assembled around them. Taste the dust from the pathways. Look at the apostles, see them pray intently and raise their hands. Feel the descent of the Holy Spirit, like a fresh gush of wind. Watch the Spirit come. Open your heart to Him. Speak to the Spirit. See Acts 8:14-17.

3. Poustinia Meditation

Unlike others methods of prayer, the task of the Poustinia Meditation *is to clear your mind of all thoughts and attempt to think of nothing other than a simple word or expression. We can remain quiet and wait for a word to be given to us, or we can select a word before our time of prayer. The* word or expression, whether given or selected, is repeated multiple times or simply held in our minds. Sometimes the use of a foreign word can help us stay focused. For our exercise today, we can use fullness, union, or zeal.

Suggested Saints and Holy Ones

As Christians, we are surrounded by "a cloud of witnesses"—the saints and holy ones in Heaven who intercede and help us. On this fourth day of our preparation, we can turn to St. Teresa Benedicta of the Cross (Edith Stein). This holy saint was born into the Jewish faith, which she abandoned the practice of as a young woman. She became a noted philosopher and professor. After meeting a Christian who lost her husband, the future saint was moved by the widow's profound faith. She knew she was lacking something in her life, so she prayed and surrendered her life to the Lord Jesus. After becoming a Catholic Christian, the Lord called her to religious life. St. Teresa Benedicta gave up her professional career and became a Carmelite Sister and a great spiritual master. She always followed wherever the Spirit led her. Because of her Jewish blood, which she always valued as a gift from God, the great saint died a martyr of charity in the Auschwitz concentration camp.

Stations of the Cross Suggestion

The Stations of the Cross are recommended. They can all be prayed or simply the Eighth Station: Jesus Admonishes the Weeping Women. Consider the Lord's counsel to the holy women to pray for their children and prepare for what is to come. Ask for the grace to weep over evil and to work for what is good and holy.

Rosary Suggestion

The Rosary is always recommended. Today, the Luminous Mysteries are suggested. In particular, the Third Mystery, the Proclamation of the Kingdom, is proposed. Reflect on the workings of the Holy Spirit in your life and in the life of the Church.

Three Traditional Prayers

Suscipe Prayer

> Take, Lord, and receive all my liberty, my memory, my understanding, and my entire will, All I have and call my own. You have given all to me. To You, Lord, I return it. Everything is Yours; do with it what You will. Give me only Your love and Your grace, that is enough for me. Amen.

Veni, Creator Spiritus

> Come, Holy Spirit, Creator blest,
> and in our souls take up Thy rest;
> come with Thy grace and heavenly aid
> to fill the hearts which Thou hast made.
>
> O comforter, to Thee we cry,
> O heavenly gift of God Most High,
> O fount of life and fire of love,
> and sweet anointing from above.
>
> Thou in Thy sevenfold gifts are known;
> Thou, finger of God's hand we own;
> Thou, promise of the Father,
> Thou Who dost the tongue with power imbue.
>
> Kindle our sense from above,
> and make our hearts o'erflow with love;
> with patience firm and virtue high
> the weakness of our flesh supply.

Far from us drive the foe we dread,
and grant us Thy peace instead;
so shall we not, with Thee for guide,
turn from the path of life aside.

Oh, may Thy grace on us bestow
the Father and the Son to know;
and Thee, through endless times confessed,
of both the eternal Spirit blest.

Now to the Father and the Son,
Who rose from death, be glory given,
with Thou, O Holy Comforter,
henceforth by all in earth and Heaven. Amen.

Prayer to Receive the Holy Spirit

O King of glory, send us the Promise of the Father, the
Spirit of Truth. May the Counselor Who proceeds from
You enlighten us and infuse all truth in us, as You have
promised. Amen.

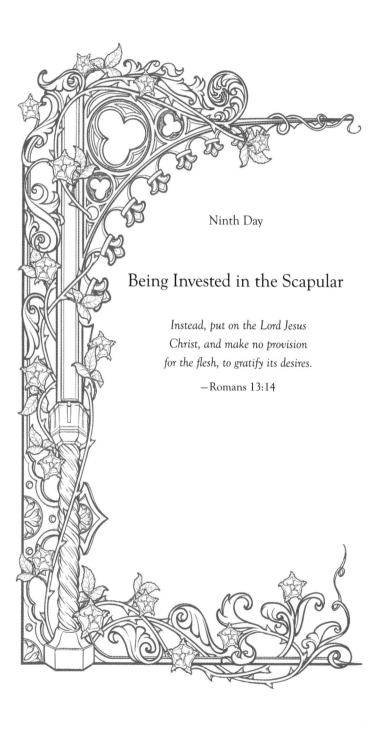

Ninth Day

Being Invested in the Scapular

*Instead, put on the Lord Jesus
Christ, and make no provision
for the flesh, to gratify its desires.*

—Romans 13:14

Preparation

As you start Day Nine, these simple preparatory acts will help you get started and keep you focused.

Today's Spiritual Goal

To understand the formula of the scapular investiture: "Receive this blessed scapular and beseech the Blessed Virgin Mary that through her merits you may wear it without stain. May it defend you against all adversity and accompany you into eternal life. Amen."

Opening Prayers

Come, Holy Spirit, fill the hearts of Your faithful. And kindle in them the fire of Your love. Send forth Your Spirit, and they shall be created. And You will renew the face of the earth.

Lord, by the light of the Holy Spirit You have taught the hearts of Your faithful. In the same Spirit, help us to relish what is right and always rejoice in Your consolation. We ask this through Christ our Lord. Amen.

We fly to your protection, O holy Mother of God. Despise not our petitions in our necessities, but deliver us always from all dangers, O glorious and blessed Virgin. Amen.

O Blessed Mother, as we prepare to be invested in your scapular, help us to be completely devoted to your Son, Jesus Christ. We rely on you. Amen.

Being Invested in the Scapular

TEACHINGS

As we observe this last day of preparation, our focus turns to our immediate readiness to be invested in the Brown Scapular of Our Lady.

As you prepare for your investiture, it is strongly recommended that you attend Mass and receive Holy Communion, especially if your investiture is going to happen outside of Mass.

Our Discipleship and the Brown Scapular

The Brown Scapular of Our Lady was given by the Blessed Virgin Mary and is a sacramental of the Church. It is a gift to help us to live and shine in our discipleship. The Scapular fans into flame the graces of our Holy Baptism and guides us to understanding what it means to live completely and unconditionally for Jesus Christ.

For those invested in the Brown Scapular, the different aspects of Christian discipleship should be zealously accepted and lived, serving as a means of holiness for themselves and those around them. Such aspects include the Holy Mass, prayer, fasting, almsgiving, and chastity.

The Gift of Holy Communion

In the Mass, as the adopted children of God, we share in the Lord's own sacrifice. As members of His Body, we join with Him as He offers everything to the Father.

We are invited to offer up our own lives with the Lord Jesus. We lift up our prayers, works, joys, and sufferings.

Flowing from the holy sacrifice, there is a memorial meal. Such a meal isn't just some casual sharing of food around some random table. This is a sacred meal, since the host and the banquet are God Himself. The Lord Jesus comes to us under the appearance of bread and wine and asks that we eat and drink his Body and Blood.

The Lord Jesus so desires a union with us that He comes to us as food. He enters into our lives, both physically and spiritually. This is an unmerited, awesome gift.

The Lord Jesus teaches us:

> I am the bread of life. Your ancestors ate the manna in the wilderness, and they died. This is the bread that comes down from heaven, so that one may eat of it and not die. I am the living bread that came down from heaven. Whoever eats of this bread will live forever; and the bread that I will give for the life of the world is my flesh. —John 6:48–51

In Holy Communion, when we eat and drink the very Body and Blood of Jesus Christ, we are united with Him. St. Paul explains such a union:

> I have been crucified with Christ; and it is no longer I who live, but it is Christ who lives in me. And the life I now live in the flesh I live by faith in the Son of God, who loved me and gave himself for me. —Galatians 2:19b–20

Yes, we are truly one with the Lord. He dwells in us and we live for Him!

By receiving the Lord Jesus in Holy Communion, we are spurred on to greater holiness. The graces of receiving Holy Communion bring about a transformation within us. Such graces wipe away our venial sins, fortify our resolve against mortal sins, build up our resistance to sensual passions, incite us to virtue, lead us to prayer and selfless service, and give us a sensitivity to the things of God and a displeasure toward sinful acts and darkness. In summary, by worthily receiving Holy Communion, we are driven to glorify God's Name, labor for His Kingdom, and generously obey His will.

Summit and Source

The Eucharist, therefore, is properly understood as the summit and source of the entire Christian way of life. Everything we do points to the Eucharist, and from the Eucharist we find the strength to do all other good things.

The Lord promised that He would not leave us orphans, and so He remains preeminently with us in the Eucharist:

> "I will not leave you orphaned; I am coming to you." —John 14:18

The Eucharist is not "extra Catholic stuff" in terms of Christian discipleship. It lies at the very heart of what it means to be a Christian. Our Baptism and Confirmation point us to the Eucharist as we seek to relive the Paschal Mystery in our lives. We see in the Eucharistic Sacrifice the sacramental re-presentation of that saving mystery—the Passion, Death, and Resurrection of Jesus Christ—and from that celebration we receive renewed vigor and strength to faithfully and zealously live as disciples of the Lord Jesus.

Eucharistic Love and the Scapular

As a Christian who is seeking to be invested in the Brown Scapular, you are particularly called to draw close our Eucharistic Lord. As someone who bears the spiritual mantle of Elijah and the Blessed Virgin Mary, you are beckoned to be a person after God's own heart. As such, you must become a close friend, an attentive listener, and a ready servant to the Lord Jesus. Such a relationship is only fully nurtured in proximity to the Eucharist.

Here are a few suggestions that can help you stay close to the Eucharistic Lord:

- ◆ Go to Confession regularly. Do not allow any grave sin to be on your heart. Fight venial sins and ask the Lord to heal you from past and strengthen you against future temptations.
- ◆ Participate devoutly in Holy Mass, not only on Sundays and Holy Days of Obligation, but also—as you're able—for daily Masses on the weekdays.
- ◆ Prepare well for Mass. Arrive early and look at the prayers and Bible readings for the Mass. Spend time in prayer preparing for Holy Communion. Offer up a longer Eucharistic fast, as you're able.
- ◆ Stay after Mass and offer up prayers of thanksgiving.
- ◆ If you cannot attend daily Mass, look at the prayers and Bible readings at home.
- ◆ Participate in Eucharistic Adoration as often as you can. This sacred prayer time is essential for intimacy with the Lord.
- ◆ Read the *Catechism of the Catholic Church*, part two, on the sacraments and the Eucharist.
- ◆ Pray the Act of Spiritual Communion often.
- ◆ Make the Sign of the Cross whenever you pass a Catholic Church.

Act of Spiritual Communion

My Jesus, I believe that You are present in the Most Holy Sacrament. I love You above all things, and I desire to receive You into my soul. Since I cannot at this moment receive You sacramentally, come at least spiritually into my heart. I embrace You as if You were already there and unite myself wholly to You. Never permit me to be separated from You. Amen.

The Scapular and the Rosary

The Christian who has been invested in the Scapular of Our Lady of Mount Carmel is to be a person who sees their relationship with the Lord Jesus through the sure lens of Mary. Such a person is called to pray, especially the Holy Rosary of Our Lady.

> Pray in the Spirit at all times in every prayer and supplication. To that end keep alert and always persevere in supplication for all the saints. — Ephesians 6:18

Such believers see the Rosary as the highest of prayers and the greatest of gifts. As such, the graces and blessings associated with the Rosary are to be a regular part of their lives. The Scapular is a sign of baptismal consecration. It is a declaration of love to Jesus and Mary. It is a commitment. It is particularly a commitment to prayer. It is the duty of praying the Holy Rosary.

It is strongly suggested that the Christian who has been invested in the Brown Scapular would, at least, pray five decades of the Rosary every day.

Suggested Morning Offering

O my God, in union with the Immaculate Heart of Mary [*here kiss your Scapular*], I offer you the Precious Blood of Jesus from all the altars throughout the world, joining with it the offering of my every thought, word, and action of this day. O my Jesus, I desire today to gain every indulgence and merit I can, and I offer them, together with myself, to Mary Immaculate, that she may best apply them to the interests of Your most Sacred Heart. Precious Blood of Jesus, save me! Immaculate Heart of Mary, pray for us! Sacred Heart of Jesus, have mercy on us! Amen.

Fasting and the Scapular

The spirituality of the Scapular, as a spirituality that heightens our baptismal consecration, cries out for fasting and other penances. The person who wears the Scapular knows that they are a sinner. They are keenly aware of their sins and the sins of humanity. They also know the tragic consequences of such sin.

> Create in me a clean heart, O God, and put a new and right spirit within me. Do not cast me away from your presence, and do not take your holy spirit from me. Restore to me the joy of your salvation, and sustain in me a willing spirit. —Psalm 51:10-12

As such, the Christian who carries Our Lady's Scapular does penance, for themselves and for our fallen world. They readily welcome the small inconveniences and annoyances throughout the day and offer them up as sacrifices to the Lord Jesus through Mary. Such believers also fast on a consistent basis. They see such fasting as a participation in the saving work of the Lord Jesus. They pray for their own salvation and that of their neighbor.

The Christian who wears the Brown Scapular is called to fast in some form, especially on the traditional penitential weekdays of Wednesday and Friday.

Being Invested in the Scapular

The Scapular and Those in Need

As Christians wear the Scapular of Our Lady, they are actively committing themselves to anyone who is in need. The simple cloth of the Scapular declares the person to be a Christian, a believer totally dedicated to Jesus Christ through Mary. As such, the ones who were close to the Lord—the poor, sick, and suffering—are also to be close to the one who fans into flame the graces of their Baptism through the Brown Scapular.

The baptized person who wears Our Lady's Scapular is summoned to serve among the lowest and least among us. It is highly recommended that some Work of Mercy be regularly offered by those who wear the scapular.

CORPORAL WORKS OF MERCY	SPIRITUAL WORKS OF MERCY
Feed the hungry.	Admonish the sinner.
Give drink to the thirsty.	Instruct the ignorant.
Clothe the naked.	Counsel the doubtful.
Visit the imprisoned.	Bear wrongs patiently.
Shelter the homeless.	Comfort the afflicted.
Visit the sick.	Forgive all injuries.
Bury the dead.	Pray for the living and dead.

Chastity and the Brown Scapular

In the spirituality surrounding it, the Brown Scapular of Our Lady is also a call to chastity according to one's state in life. Chastity is to be a virtue of all the baptized. It is the ordering of our sexual desires according to truth and love. It places our sexual powers within our vocation as the children of God.

Since the scapular is literally worn on our bodies, it is a summons to recognize our bodies as gifts from God and temples of the Holy Spirit.

> Or do you not know that your body is a temple of the Holy Spirit within you, which you have from God, and that you are not your own? For you were bought with a price; therefore glorify God in your body. — 1 Corinthians 6:19-20

Those who wear the Scapular of Our Lady, therefore, are invited to cherish and live a noble chastity according to their state in life.

Being Invested in the Scapular

SPIRITUAL EXERCISES

For the spiritual preparation of this final day, it is recommended that you pray and reflect upon your baptismal promises.

Baptismal Promises

℣: Do you renounce sin, so as to live in the freedom of the children of God?

℟: I do.

℣: Do you renounce the lure of evil, so that sin may have no mastery over you?

℟: I do.

℣: Do you renounce Satan, the author and prince of sin?

℟: I do.

℣: Do you believe in God, the Father Almighty, Creator of Heaven and earth?

℟: I do.

℣: Do you believe in Jesus Christ, His only Son, our Lord, Who was born of the Virgin Mary, suffered death and was buried, rose again from the dead and is seated at the right hand of the Father?

℟: I do.

Conclusion

The Ceremony of the Investiture in the Brown Scapular of Our Lady of Mount Carmel[1]

Priest: Show us, O Lord, Your mercy.
Respondent: And grant us Your salvation.

P: Lord, hear my prayer.
R: And let my cry come You.
P: The Lord be with you.
R: And with your Spirit.
P: Lord Jesus Christ, Savior of the human race, sanctify by Your power these Scapulars, which for love of You and for love of Our Lady of Mount Carmel, Your servants will wear devoutly, so that through the intercession of the same Virgin Mary, Mother of God, and protected against the evil spirit, they

---

[1]   As provided by the Carmelite Monastery of the Sacred Hearts, Colorado Springs, Colorado.

persevere until death in your grace. You who live and reign world without end. Amen.

The priest sprinkles the scapulars with holy water.

P: Receive this blessed Scapular and beseech the Blessed Virgin that through her merits, you may wear it without stain. May it defend you against all adversity and accompany you to eternal life. Amen.

The priest invests the person.

P: By the power vested in me, I admit you to participate in all the spiritual benefits obtained through the mercy of Jesus Christ by the Religious Order of Mount Carmel. In the Name of the Father and of the Son ✠ and of the Holy Spirit. Amen.

The priest then offers a blessing:

May God Almighty, the Creator of Heaven and earth, bless ✠ you, He Who has deigned to join you to the Confraternity of the Blessed Virgin of Mount Carmel; we beseech her to crush the head of the ancient serpent so that you may enter into possession of your eternal heritage through Christ our Lord.

R: Amen.

The priest then sprinkles the person with his or her scapular on.

Bibliography

General Sources

Holy Bible. New Revised Standard Version: Catholic Edition. Washington, DC: National Council of the Churches of Christ in the United States of America, 1989, 1993.

Catechism of the Catholic Church, 2nd ed. Washington, DC: Libreria Editrice Vaticana–United States Conference of Catholic Bishops, 2000.

John Paul II. Encyclical *Redemptoris Missio* (December 7, 1990).

Primary Sources

Dolan, Albert. *Scapular Facts*. N.p. Carmelite Press, 1929.

Dubay, Thomas. *Fire Within: Saint Teresa, Saint John of the Cross, and the Gospel on Prayer*. San Francisco: Ignatius Press, 1989.

Haffert, John. *Mary in Her Scapular Promise*. Colorado Springs: Sisters of Mount Carmel, 2011.

Kirby, Jeffrey. *Glory Unto Glory*. Brooklyn, NY: Angelico Press, 2022.

———. *Lord, Teach Us to Pray*. Charlotte, NC: Saint Benedict Press, 2014.

———. *Manual for Suffering*. Charlotte, NC: TAN Books, 2021.

———. *Thy Kingdom Come*. Charlotte, NC: TAN Books, 2020.

Appendix A

Optional Holy Days for Investiture

Starting Date	Marian Feast	Feast Day
February 3	Our Lady of Lourdes	February 11
March 17	The Annunciation	March 25
May 5	Our Lady of Fatima	May 13
May 23	The Visitation	May 31
Varies	Immaculate Heart	Saturday after Corpus Christi
July 8	Our Lady of Mt. Carmel	July 16
August 7	The Assumption	August 15
August 14	Queenship of Mary	August 22
August 31	Nativity of Mary	September 8
September 4	Holy Name of Mary	September 12
September 7	Our Lady of Sorrows	September 15
September 29	Our Lady of the Rosary	October 7

A Journey to Mount Carmel

Starting Date	Marian Feast	Feast Day
November 13	Presentation of Mary	November 21
November 30	Immaculate Conception	December 8
December 4	Our Lady of Guadalupe	December 12
December 24	Mother of God	January 1
January 25	Presentation of the Lord	February 2

Appendix B

Questions and Answers on the Brown Scapular

How must the scapular be worn?

The scapular is worn over the shoulders, so that one part hangs over your chest and the other side hangs over the back. Both parts cannot be carried in the front or the back.

May the Scapular be pinned to my clothing?

Yes, the scapular may be pinned to an undergarment to keep it from rising about a person's neck.

Does the Scapular have to be wool?

Yes, the scapular must be wool. Other material is not permitted.

What if I'm allergic to wool?

If a person has a serious allergy to wool or has irritation of the skin, the scapular can be worn over clothing, covered in plastic, or a Scapular Medal can be used.

The Scapular Medal, then, can be a replacement for the scapular?

The Scapular Medal can only be used for serious reasons, such as an allergy to wool. As the Carmelite Religious always wear their full scapulars, so the laity and secular priests who are invested in the scapular should always seek to wear their scapular.

Are there set images that must be on the scapular?

So long as the scapular itself is brown, any images are permitted, although it is customary to have Our Lady of Mount Carmel on one side and the Carmelite shield on the other.

Does the scapular always have to be worn?

Other than showering, the scapular must always be worn. It cannot be removed for reasons of convenience or vanity.

If I need a new scapular, do I need to be reinvested?

If your scapular has worn out or has broken, you only need to get a new one. Your investiture is still valid.

What is the Sabbatine Privilege?

The Sabbatine Privilege is the promise of the Blessed Virgin Mary that she will deliver anyone who devoutly died wearing the scapular from Purgatory soon after their death, especially the first Saturday after death.

About the Author

Fr. Jeffrey Kirby, S.T.D., is a moral theologian, a leader in adult formation programs, and the pastor of Our Lady of Grace Parish in Indian Land, South Carolina. He is a Papal Missionary of Mercy and an adjunct professor of theology at Belmont Abbey College. Fr. Kirby is the author of several books, including *Understanding the Bible: A Catholic Guide to Applying God's Word to Your Life Today* and *Sanctify Them in Truth: How the Church's Social Doctrine Addresses the Issues of Our Time*.

Sophia Institute

Sophia Institute is a nonprofit institution that seeks to nurture the spiritual, moral, and cultural life of souls and to spread the gospel of Christ in conformity with the authentic teachings of the Roman Catholic Church.

Sophia Institute Press fulfills this mission by offering translations, reprints, and new publications that afford readers a rich source of the enduring wisdom of mankind.

Sophia Institute also operates the popular online resource CatholicExchange.com. *Catholic Exchange* provides world news from a Catholic perspective as well as daily devotionals and articles that will help readers to grow in holiness and live a life consistent with the teachings of the Church.

In 2013, Sophia Institute launched Sophia Institute for Teachers to renew and rebuild Catholic culture through service to Catholic education. With the goal of nurturing the spiritual, moral, and cultural life of souls, and an abiding respect for the role and work of teachers, we strive to provide materials and programs that are at once enlightening to the mind and ennobling to the heart; faithful and complete, as well as useful and practical.

Sophia Institute gratefully recognizes the Solidarity Association for preserving and encouraging the growth of our apostolate over the course of many years. Without their generous and timely support, this book would not be in your hands.

www.SophiaInstitute.com
www.CatholicExchange.com
www.SophiaInstituteforTeachers.org

Sophia Institute Press is a registered trademark of Sophia Institute.
Sophia Institute is a tax-exempt institution as defined by the
Internal Revenue Code, Section 501(c)(3). Tax ID 22-2548708.